TO KNOW

TO KNOW

A Guide to

Women's Magic

and

Spirituality

BY JADE

DELPHI PRESS, INC.

Oak Park, Illinois

Born July 2, 1950, Jade has a Cancer sun, an Aquarius Moon and Gemini rising. She was born in Ohio and grew up in Kentucky, where in 1975 she found both the women's movement and women's religion. Since 1982 Jade has lived in Wisconsin where she and Lynnie Levy founded the Re-formed Congregation of the Goddess, a legally incorporated, tax-exempt religious organization, and Of a Like Mind, a network and newspaper for Goddess women.

People often ask Jade how she managed to write a book while raising a teen-age son and working full-time for the Congregation. Her most frequent reply is that her house is never quite as clean as it could be.

Published 1991 by Delphi Press, Inc., Oak Park, Illinois, 60304

© 1991 by Samantha Jade River

95 94 93 92 91   5 4 3 2 1

Manufactured in the United States of America

Library of Congress Catalogue Number: 90-82977

ISBN 1-878980-00-9

Contents

To Falcon who believes in the magic,
to Lynnie who believes in the dream,
and to Normajean who believes in me.

Acknowledgements

My grateful thanks go to Daña and Lynnie whose tireless editing and insightful comments helped this book be the best that it could be.

My loving appreciation goes to Normajean whose many hours of work brought the manuscript together and to Casey for his patience with having a mother who is writing a book.

My sincere gratitude goes to the Consistery of the Re-formed Congregation of the Goddess for their support and encouragement.

Introduction

Women are spiritual beings. Deep within each woman lies an under-standing, a spiritual core that has defied all attempts to silence it. Infor-mation about women's spiritual truths has long been suppressed. Fear, misunderstanding, and a lack of information have kept women from seeking and sharing spiritual knowledge with each other. Despite this, women's spiritual truths have emerged both in cultures which sup-ported and encouraged women in their spiritual quests and in cultures where speaking this truth was punishable by death. Within the com-munity of womanspirit, women are daring to speak their truths—to question, explore, define, and develop what it means to be a spiritual woman in today's world. Some of the answers are ancient, and some are brand new. This new women's spirituality is more than the old re-ligions which are its basis. It incorporates diverse beliefs from multiple sources which include Celtic Wicca, Shamanism, Native American, Greek, and Roman traditions, science fiction, and feminism, but it ex-tends beyond all of these to form the basis of a new religion which speaks to the lives of women in this time.

Many of the beliefs and practices of this new religion are based on the principles of magic. Magic within the community of womanspirit has nothing to do with sleight-of-hand. It is a mindful state of active participation in creating reality. In women's spirituality there is a con-cept of creation as an intelligent whole. Magic is seen as the mechanism which we can use to communicate with this intelligence. Women's rituals, divination, and spells are some of the magical tools that are used to form and observe time, space, and matter.

Traditionally, four things are required to do magic: to know, to will, to dare, and to keep the silence. This book answers the first requirement by sharing with women what they need "to know" in order to find the magic within themselves. This is not a how-to book. You will not find any psychic exercises, ritual outlines or spellcraft on the following pages. Instead there is a compilation of information that answers some of the most commonly asked questions about women's, feminist, and Pagan spirituality. In this book one will find practical information about women's spirituality along with resources which can help access this prolific underground community.

Today there are thousands of women who call themselves Witches. Why a woman would choose to identify with such a title, and what would lead her to feel that the word Witch would truly describe a positive spiritual path, is often a mystery to those attempting to find information about women's spiritual beliefs. The Craft, as Witchcraft is often called by those who practice it, has a longstanding tradition of silence. Women who have chosen to celebrate and practice a woman-centered spirituality through the ages have often been exploited, oppressed, and destroyed as a result. Silence was the way of the wise who wished to survive to pass the traditions of women on to their daughters and grandchildren. This tradition of silence still holds true for many of those who practice women's Witchcraft, and finding information about the women's spiritual community can be challenging. Much of the material which is available to date describes portions of the Craft without giving a cohesive picture of the actual practice, thealogy and beliefs of spiritual women. *To Know* speaks about the women's spiritual community and how to find it. It also details and documents a worldwide women's religious movement.

Many of the chapters which follow contain both information and resources. In the text of each chapter you may notice asterisks (*). These asterisks mean that resource information about this person, group, or other source is included in the resource section of that chapter. For those of you who want to find and make contact with others in the sometimes elusive community of womanspirit, these are your keys. As all facets of women's spirituality seem to overlap, these chapters are divided into somewhat arbitrary categories. It may, therefore, be important to check to see if the information that you are looking for is covered in another chapter.

This book is intended to serve as a guide for those who want to live as spiritual women. It is a handbook which contains the information, advice, suggestions, inspiration, examples, hints, and cautions that can lead you on your journey into womanspirit. Whether you are just beginning your journey or have been traveling on a spiritual path for many years, may this book awaken within you your own knowledge and inner truth and lead you "to know" that the world of womanspirit is a world of limitless possibilities.

CHAPTER 1

A History of the Women's Spiritual Movement

- *The Women's Movement and Women's Religion—*
  The Early Realizations

There are many paths to women's religion, but the most common of these seems to be the women's movement itself. The women's movement has been a fertile source for a new generation and genre of Witches, Goddess Worshippers, and Pagans. Women's spirituality, as it is most often called, has brought forth innovative and motivated Witches who have emerged as a strong force within the feminist and Pagan communities.

The consciousness-raising group was one of the most powerful tools of communication in the early women's movement. Women came together to share the feelings and insights they found in common. Sometimes this was a very formal process organized by a particular group with a regular meeting time and a set group of women, and sometimes it was just a group of friends who met together around the kitchen table whenever they got the chance. During this process, women discovered that they shared "spiritual" feelings. These were, however, vague and undefined. Women felt connected to the earth, to the moon, to the seasons, and to each other, but they lacked a way to express exactly what that meant.

Although some feminists were practicing within traditional religious systems, many more did not feel validated by traditional religious alternatives. Women who had made decisions to continue to participate in traditional religion often compromised by ignoring a large part of the religious doctrine. Many times women who could not accept traditional religion decided to ignore their "spiritual feelings" rather than accept any traditional religion and its seemingly oppressive attitudes toward women. They became agnostics or atheists.

In consciousness-raising groups, women shared stories of the effects of their religious upbringings. Whether they were raised Protestant, Catholic, Jewish, or in a less well known religion, a common theme emerged. The traditional religious options offered by our society did not seem to fit with their "spiritual feelings." They talked of how it felt to be offered a spiritual system that had no concept of the female as divine. They explored their feelings about the notion of original sin and the role of women in traditional religion. They puzzled over the idea of male superiority offered by these religions and looked for the source of the "divine proof" for this theory. They studied religious texts and looked into alternative religions.

A frightening realization emerged from this process. Women found that they were oppressed by traditional religion. A foundation of the oppression was often found in the beliefs and practices of the religions with which we had been raised. This was not something that was easy to confront. It is difficult to convey the personal confusion that this realization caused many women. It appeared that the entire traditional religious system that our society had taught us as children had to be re-evaluated within the framework of a feminist consciousness.

■ Unlearning

It was not enough to simply re-evaluate what we had been taught within traditional religion about women and the resulting social attitudes; we were now faced with the difficult task of re-interpreting these teachings. Sifting and winnowing the facts from the fables, we tried to unlearn the morals and dogma that were embedded within our culture and ourselves. Everything needed to be re-evaluated, from fairy tales to the protestant work ethic, and to be judged from the perspective of women's experience, to determine if it was still valid. Attitudes, values, and beliefs found not to be in keeping with women's experience had to be unlearned, and women had to look deep within themselves for their own truths.

With this realization, some women retreated back into traditional religion rather than look any further. Others, however, were now truly curious. Where did the attitudes about women that were conveyed in traditional religion come from? If one were to replace traditional religion with a feminist ethic, thealogy (women's theology), and philosophy, what would it be like? Were there any examples of feminist religions? What happens when religion includes a concept of a female deity?

These questions were ones for which there were no ready answers. It appeared as if few had ever asked them before or, if they had, the answers had either never been recorded or had not survived. Literature on these topics could not be easily obtained, and there were few sources for spiritual insight outside traditional religious thought. Regardless of these limited resources, women began to search what literature and information they could find, and gradually a pattern began to emerge.

Many Native American cultures were based on a system that honored women and recognized elder women as appropriate decision makers. The Greek myths held examples of strong women Goddesses who filled many different roles. The Celtic cultures of the British Isles were filled with tales of women warriors and leaders. The lands overrun in biblical times were not uninhabited, and it seemed that women had a different place in those cultures. It appeared that clues of what women's culture and religion could truly be like lay in the past. Modern women had discovered the matriarchy. It became clear that many of the values taught by traditional religion were based on a response to a matriarchal system that seemed nearly global in its scope.

These discoveries only caused women to ask more questions. What was matriarchy? What did it mean? How did it work? Women discovered that other women had asked the same questions before. Matilda Joslyn Gage, a suffragist, in her book *Woman, Church, and State** had also discovered what she referred to as the Matriarchate. She states ". . . records prove that women had acquired great liberty under the old civilizations. A form of society existed at an early age known as the Matriarchate or Mother-rule."[1] The works of J. J. Bachofen also gave hints about the nature of this ancient women's culture. Bachofen's *Myth, Religion, and Mother Right,** first published in 1954, gave tantalizing glimpses of matriarchal thought and social structure. This was one of the first books about matriarchy to be recognized by the scholarly community (perhaps because it was written by a man). It started a scholarly debate, which still continues, about the validity of the existence of matriarchal culture.

The work of Elizabeth Gould Davis and her book *The First Sex** emerged within women's circles at this time, almost as if in answer to these questions. Although traditional authorities of higher education questioned her scholarship, for women who were seeking information about woman-centered culture and religion, this book was a wonderful affirmation. Groups of women read it and discussed it together. The ideas and thoughts that this book presented were so different from traditional concepts that for many women it was a challenge to read and comprehend. The process of unlearning had truly begun. If we looked at history as herstory and considered interpretations of the past from a feminist and woman-centered perspective, then the answers that we found were entirely different from those that we had been taught.

The process of unlearning now took on a new dimension. If there had truly been a woman-oriented spirituality before, what happened to it? Why did our culture not acknowledge it? What had happened to the matriarchy? It became clear that there was a tremendous cover-up about the role of women in early cultures. Women began blowing the dust off of old books and scholarship about the matriarchy, and the role of women's spirituality in the distant past became an area of feminist study. What emerged was more frightening than anything that had yet been discovered. The evidence was overwhelming that the matriarchy had been willfully destroyed. With the emergence of male-dominated religions, female deities and the more women-centered cultures had been conquered.

In 1976 Merlin Stone's book, *When God was a Woman,** answered these questions in chilling detail. Stone tells of the conquest of the matriarchies of the fertile crescent. These matriarchies were, Stone asserts, largely vegetarian. She details that matriarchal societies were agrarian and lacked skills in warfare. Stone explains that most of the matriarchal cultures placed a great value on life. Because of this cultural value, they were hesitant hunters and did not develop the hunting skills that could be translated into warfare. As such, the matriarchies became easy prey for the patriarchal tribes who invaded from the northern steppes of Europe. These tribes brought with them both their skills in weaponry and their belief in a stern father god.

Stone goes on to explain the process of change that began as a result of these conquests. With the invasions from the north came many changes in the religions and the attitudes of the people of the fertile crescent. The strong Goddess figures who had predominated the religious beliefs of the matriarchies were assigned new personalities, characteristics, and sexual preferences. Their roles became submissive to the strong male deities. Goddesses who were thought by the invaders to be too strongly identified with what they viewed as male characteristics were co-opted or metamorphosed into male or bisexual deities. After these changes, the Goddesses of the matriarchy who still posed a threat to the new order were turned into devils or killed by the new "heroes" or married to male deities. This, Stone explains, was not an immediate change but was a slow amalgamation of matriarchal thought and religion with those of the invading tribes. This process varied greatly from place to place and in the amount of time that it took for the matriarchal social structure to be absorbed or eliminated from the emerging culture.

■ The Matriarchy Goes Underground

This information was a wonderful affirmation of women's past spiritual traditions, but at the same time it created an atmosphere of sadness and confusion. Was that all? Had women's spiritual thought simply vanished with the matriarchies? Women had uncovered information about other women-centered spiritualities, but little actual information about the religious and spiritual practices of the matriarchy remained. Were women left to begin again? Why had so little matriarchal thought survived?

The northern invaders with their strong concept of a male deity and proscriptive behavioral codes had a difficult time converting and conforming the matriarchal peoples. The matriarchies had a permissive behavioral code and were reluctant to give up the freedoms that they had enjoyed. They were even more reluctant to give up their Goddesses. These Goddesses were an influential part of the lives of the matriarchal peoples and were almost impossible to erase. If god was to replace the Goddess, drastic measures were needed.

The actual invasion and conquering of the matriarchal peoples was one of the strongest measures. In many areas, entire populations of cities were killed. Often the only persons who were spared were girls assumed young enough to be virgins. Naturally, it was difficult for these young survivors to remember the cultural attitudes of their mothers, much less carry them on. Elimination of large segments of the matriachal population was, of course, an effective means of ensuring that the matriarchy would not emerge as a force again.

In cases where the takeover was less complete, a more insidious form of psychological warfare began. The early patriarchs began an attempt to establish the belief that if the Goddesses of the matriarchy were stronger than the gods of the patriarchs, they would not have allowed their people to be conquered. A general maligning and oppression of matriarchal thought occured in both culture and myth. The subjugation of women and the resulting theological basis for their oppression was further developed. The beliefs and thoughts of these early patriarchs are the foundation of both Jewish and Christian morality and theology that is still the pervading influence in our western religious thought today. Any woman or man who strongly opposed this theological/governmental philosophy was executed. This remained true up until the 1800s.

Despite these overwhelming circumstances, searching feminists found that matriarchal thought had emerged again and again. In some cases, as in the British Isles, it had never been effectively suppressed. It appeared that matriarchal spirituality had gone underground because of the danger to the practitioners. It became clear, in fact, that matriarchal thought and spiritual information had survived as an oral tradition and that this oral tradition was what we had been taught to call as Witchcraft. The woman-centered Goddesses of the old religions had been defined by patriarchy as the devils and demons of Christianity and Judaism. This was a staggering revelation. Many women were not prepared to deal with the ramifications of this discovery. Serious unlearning would have to take place if modern feminists were to think of themselves as Witches. There were many women who could not or did not wish to make the transition from their old, comfortable forms of thought and behavior to the dangerous ground of declaring themselves as Witches in solidarity with the matriarchy. To reject traditional religion was one thing, but to replace it with something so radical was quite another. It was especially difficult to replace it with something with such strong, negative connotations in the present culture.

The sociological studies of Margaret Murray* in her books *The God of the Witches* and *The Witch Cult in Western Europe* detailed the link between the previously existing matriarchal religious structure and the Witchcraft practices of Celtic Europe. Although greatly disputed in scholarly circles, the work of Murray only confirmed that, in fact, matriarchal religion was really closely related to what had come to be known as Witchcraft.

■ *The Emergence of Wicca as Women's Religion*

It seemed that each time one set of questions about women's spirituality was answered, another set of questions emerged. If matriarchal religion had become Witchcraft, what was Witchcraft all about? What were the ethics and practices of the Craft, and, judged from a feminist perspective, how was Witchcraft different from what we had been taught?

Once again women began dusting off old books in an attempt to uncover more information about Witches. What they found was truly a pleasant surprise to many. Thinking through what we had been taught about Witches and finding information available about them with a feminist view, the information began to take on new meaning. Witches generally were persecuted for one or more of the following reasons: 1) they were beautiful; 2) they were ugly; 3) they were assertive and outspoken; 4) they took responsibility for themselves and their own healthcare; 5) they owned property; 6) often they were women who lived alone or in the company of other women (including lesbians); 7) they did not meet or accept cultural standards; 8) they celebrated their own power and challenged or ignored political systems which did not serve them. Looking at Witches from this perspective, they seemed like pioneer feminist sisters suffering in a system equally, if not more, oppressive than the one in which we were struggling.

If Witches were, in fact, only women who were living feminist principles, what had caused the generations of bad press? Back in the consciousness-raising groups, which by now had turned into spirituality groups, women acknowledged that just being a feminist who challenged the system could have been enough. Others pointed out that, until only about 200 years ago, religion and government were one and the same and that to challenge one was to undermine the other. Still that did not seem to account for the strength of the feelings our culture had taught us about Witches.

When searching for information about Witchcraft, feminists found that information about all kinds of other subjects was mixed in, seemingly as a part of the Craft. Particularly, there was information about Satanism mixed in with information about Witchcraft. Witchcraft often seemed to be considered synonymous with Satanism in the information that was available to them. Ah, but we were ready for this one. If the Goddesses of the matriarchy were seen by the emerging patriarchy to be devils, then of course it could be easy to confuse Satanism and

Witchcraft and to consider them to be the same religion. But were they? With some study, it became clear that the practices of Satanism were decidedly Christian. Black Masses were carried out by defrocked priests, crosses were hung upside down and spat upon, the Lord's Prayer was said backwards. It appeared that to be a Satanist one must strongly hold to Christian ritual and teachings. Feminists had already studied Christian teachings and had learned that they had little to do with validating feminist thought, and so it became obvious that women's spirituality had nothing to do with Satanism. Feminist Witches were not Satanists. Having cleared that hurdle, feminists continued searching.

The Feminist Book of Lights and Shadows,* (now titled *The Holy Book of Women's Mysteries*), by Z. Budapest, was first published in 1976. This was, for many women, their first encounter with Feminist Witchcraft. Budapest was raised in Hungary by her mother and grandmother who were both Witches. She became a feminist after coming to the United States and forged together the basics of a hereditary Craft tradition and modern feminism. *The Feminist Book of Lights and Shadows* answered many questions about the practice of Witchcraft that women had been asking. It gave information about the celebration of women's religion, the tools of the Craft, the Craft calendar, holidays, spells, herbs, and more. This book became the starting point for many a feminist coven and a guide for newcomers to the women's Craft.

Roadblocks within the Women's Movement

During this same period of questioning and discovery, women learned the value of political organization and action. They also began to perceive how much their every-day activities affected their lives. Women sought change both through political means and by changing their attitudes and actions in their own daily lives. The personal was political. It was here that the women's movement came to a crossroads.

Having been raised in a culture that included a dichotomy between the spiritual and the secular, many women felt that the emerging spiritual side of the women's movement was a threat. Some women believed that political action was the best medium for social change and that women's spirituality was a diversion that absorbed some of the most dedicated and forceful sisters. Those active in women's spirituality and political action both, however, believed that political action alone could not have a lasting effect. The underlying ethics, myths, and morals of traditional religion must be re-examined and re-defined to give a basis for political action.

This was not a new issue. During the suffrage movement in the late 1800s Matilda Joslyn Gage was a strong advocate for re-evaluation of Christianity and investigation of the matriarchy. In her book *Woman, Church, and State*, the introduction explains the almost complete deletion of Gage's participation in the suffrage movement by her contemporaries, Susan B. Anthony and Elizabeth Cady Stanton. This was due to her insistence that religion was a women's issue.

For some new feminist Witches there was a brief period in which their political activities declined, but most returned shortly to their political activites with a renewed energy. They were full of creative ways to address all types of problems within the women's movement, from the interpersonal to the international. They brought with them spells to heal the spirit and rituals to heal the earth. They taught new ways of looking at the world and life-affirming, woman-centered forms of organization. In 1982, Starhawk articulated in *Dreaming the Dark** what political Witches had been saying all along. Spirituality is a strong basis upon which to organize for social change.

Although there are still those who see women's spirituality as a contemplative religion which will pull women out of serious political work, most women active in political work have come to recognize that the women's movement must have a soul and that women must have a form of spiritual expression that validates their political work. A bond has been formed between women working for social change and spiritual women, for in many cases these women are one in the same. Today women's spirituality is seeing a tremendous rise in interest, while the traditional women's movement, which disavowed the concept of woman's spirituality, seems to have almost burned itself out. Hopefully, it is the same spiritual women who were at first thought suspect for their spirituality who will bring new enthusiasm to the women's political movements of the future.

■ Other Routes to Women's Spirituality

There are routes, other than the women's movement, which have led women to an acceptance of Witchcraft and Goddess religions. In the same spirit of social action as the women's movement, women joined the environmental movement. The women who participated in ecology-based activities came to understand the basics of feminist re-

ligion from one of its best teachers, the Earth herself. These women began to feel a connection to the Earth and her cycles, to understand the
importance of maintaining the balance of existing eco-systems, and to
know the power of the Earth to generate and maintain life. This led
many of them to an almost reverential awe of the Earth. These women,
too, began to search for a religious system that validated these feelings.
Many of them followed a path parallel to the feminists in their search
for an alternative religion. Environmentalists searched within traditional religion for validation of their activities with little success. The
biblical verse from Genesis 2:28, "Be fruitful, and multiply, and fill the
earth, and subdue it,"[2] seemed to be the functioning injunction in the
traditional religions' relationships to the Earth. As one might suspect,
this led these women environmentalists to question the dominant par-
adigm that they had been taught, and eventually to unlearn traditional
ideas about the forms and structures of reality. Finally, for many, this
led to an acceptance of Witchcraft and women's spirituality as their
own religion.

Another road to women's spirituality which may seem unusual is
through science fiction and fantasy. For the readers of speculative fiction in the women's movement, in the environmental movement, and
for others alone in their living rooms, speculative fiction was setting
the stage for their search and acceptance of women's religion. It may at
first seem odd that a certain type of fictional reading could lend itself
toward alternative religion; however, a look at science fiction and particularly fantasy can help explain how the values contained in women's
religion could be developed.

Many science fantasy novels have an acceptance of magic. Magic
features strongly as an integral part of many fantasy story lines. The
effects of both good and negative magic are seen clearly, and even
minor characters often carry some small magic skill or lament their lack
thereof. In women's religion, magic forms a major thread. Energy directed toward a positive end constitutes the major work of both group
and individual women's rituals.

Further, speculative fiction is often filled with Goddesses. Occasionally, an actual Goddess or two makes an appearance, but even more
prevalent is the characters' acceptance of the Goddess as a part of their
lives. Many fantasy books have repeated references to a Goddess.
Characters speak of Her, swear by Her, and discuss the karma of the
situation in which they find themselves.

Science fiction and fantasy both encourage alternative views of reality. They present many possible world views which assist the reader to look at life in different ways. Regular readers of speculative fiction are often more willing to consider a world view outside that which traditional society has offered. These alternative ideas which form the fabric of much of science fiction's best tales also form an alternative view and a wider acceptance of differing beliefs and lifestyles among science fiction readers. Upon emerging from their books, some science fiction readers began searching for a world that contained some of the values that they had grown to know. Fantasy kept the magic alive for these women, and they found women's religion a welcome haven which shared their beliefs.

Most feminist Witches began to agree that women's religion is not new, but has been with us since pre-Christian days, when it was the predominant religion. Women sought a feminist alternative and rediscovered the old Goddess religions. Drawing from these sources and their own instinctive knowledge, women remembered and created their own ethics, thealogy, rituals, and philosophy: a feminist religion that is celebratory and life-affirming, that honors the cycles of the Earth and the cycles of women themselves.

■ Recommended Reading

Elizabeth Gould Davis, *The First Sex*. Baltimore: Penguin Books, Inc., 1971.

Merlin Stone, *When God was a Woman*. New York: The Dial Press, 1976.

Starhawk, *Dreaming the Dark: Magic, Sex, & Politics*. Boston: Beacon Press, 1982.

Matilda Joslyn Gage, *Woman, Church, and State*. Persephone Press: Watertown, Massachusetts, 1980.

■ Resources

Z. Budapest, *The Feminist Book of Lights and Shadows*. Venice, CA: Luna Publications, 1976. Now available in an expanded edition as *The Holy Book of Women's Mysteries*. Berkeley, CA: Wingbow Press, 1989.

Margaret A. Murray, *The God of the Witches*. New York: Oxford University Press, 1979.

Margaret A. Murray, *The Witch Cult in Western Europe*. New York: Oxford University Press, 1979.

J. J. Bachofen, *Myth, Religion, and Mother Right*. Princeton: Princeton University Press, 1967.

■ *Notes*

1. Matilda Joslyn Gage, *Woman, Church, and State*. Watertown, Massachusetts: Persephone Press, 1980, p. 8.

2. *The Bible*, New Scofield Reference Edition. New York: Oxford University Press, 1967, p. 12.

CHAPTER 2

The Thealogy

of

Women's

Witchcraft

For thousands of years there have been theologians: men who study the relationship of God to man and to the universe. This has been an area of study which simply by its language has precluded the total participation of women. This is not to say that there have not been women theologians, simply that those who would declare themselves so had to disagree quietly and/or consent to participate in the study of a male god and the presumed connection to his chosen people in the universe, men.

Many women are no longer content defining divinity in male terms and are exploring the connection between their deity and themselves. There is an emergence of thealogy, the study of the Goddess and Her connection to the universe. Drawn from the name of the Greek Goddess Thea, thealogy is the name used to describe the emerging philosophy of women's religion.

There is no overall accepted philosophy or thealogy of women's spirituality or women's Wicca, but there are areas of agreement and some areas which are still being discussed and defined. In 1979 I wrote the "Affirmation of ♀'s Spirituality" as an expression of a personal thealogy. This Affirmation became part of the foundation of the Re-formed Congregation of the Goddess and *Of a Like Mind*, an international newspaper and network of spiritual women. To be a member of either the Congregation or *Of a Like Mind* women sign the Affirmation as a statement of faith (not a test of faith) and also state that they consider themselves on a positive path of spiritual growth.

■ *Affirmation of ♀'s Spirituality*

There is one circle of ♀'s energy, and I,_____, am a part of this energy and it is mine to direct. I wish to direct this energy. . .

To Know:

- That I can create my own reality and that sending out a positive expectation will bring a positive result;
- That the energy which I send out returns to me;
- That there are an infinite number of possibilities for my life;
- That every situation is an opportunity to practice and develop my craft;
- That my instincts and intuition can be used to guide me;
- That my only power is in the present;
- That the Goddess or life force energy is within me.

To Will:

- That I shall try never to use my energy unwisely or to limit the free will of another;
- That I shall grow in wisdom, strength, knowledge, and understanding;
- That I shall, as much as I am aware, act in honesty to myself and to others;
- That I shall never use my energy for what I know to be evil, aggressive or manipulative, and shall only use my energy for what I know to be positive ends;
- That I shall grow to understand the cyclic, life affirming rhythms of the earth, and will always act with love toward her and all her plants and creatures;
- That I shall transform all negative in my environment.

To Dare:

- To be myself;
- To take responsibility for myself and my actions and know that consciously or unconsciously, I have drawn situations to me;
- To be strong and independent even in the midst of struggle;
- To accept and understand those whose ethnic or racial background, social or economic class, appearance, or sexual preference are different from my own;

–To stand firm and committed to ♀ and my spiritual beliefs even in times of isolation, pain, desperation or negativity.

And to understand when to speak and when to keep silence. So Mote it be.

To date, this Affirmation has been accepted by hundreds of women, in the Re-formed Congregation and Of a Like Mind and as such, it is a representative thealogy of women's Wicca. It does, however, coexist with many other thealogies, both very similar and extremely diverse. As one will be able to observe throughout this book, the definitions, practices, and philosophy of women's spirituality are extremely individual. A belief basic to all feminist Craft teaching is that each individual is responsible for discovering and enacting her own truth. This means that interpretation of the Craft (along with everything else in one's life) is individually determined. It would be a gross violation of the most basic of Craft principles to attempt to dictate the beliefs of another. This commitment to individual responsibility extends even into thealogy, implying that each woman's thealogical views can be personally determined.

I would like to stress that no thealogy should be accepted without identification and evaluation of one's own feelings and personal values. The Bahá'is teach the independent investigation of truth and, especially when determining a personal thealogy, it is imperative that one apply this principle. This chapter will, of course, present information from a personal thealogy which contains some bias. In the interest of allowing the independent investigation of truth, information from other thealogies will also be presented. Listen for what rings true to you, and begin or continue your own investigation.

Because the Affirmation of ♀'s Spirituality is a representative thealogy of women's Wicca, the principles it contains are used as a springboard for this chapter.

■ The Goddess

"The Goddess or Life Force Energy Is Within Me"

One may wonder what assumptions underlie a thealogy which is so individually defined. In traditional religions there are assumptions that order must be imposed from without; that people are by nature sinful and if left to their own devices will commit all types of hedonistic or criminal acts which would be to the detriment of society as a whole. This assumption of sinfulness and the resulting unsocialized behavior is in direct conflict with the most basic Wiccan belief; the belief that the Goddess, or an individualization of the energy which comprises Her, is carried in each of us.

One of the most basic skills of the Craft is to learn how to connect with the Goddess within and to identify knowledge that comes from this source. The awareness of this knowledge provides direction and connection to an "inner knowing." This inner knowing has many names depending primarily upon which area of your body you receive this signal from. Inner bell, deep truth, gut feeling, instinct, intuition, little voices, psychic sense, and hunch are all ways to describe identifying and connecting with the information that comes from the spark of the Goddess within.

"My Instincts and Intuition Can Be Used to Guide Me"

Goddess/lifeforce energy can be used as a guide when one is in touch with it. There is no activity, decision, or action that is too insignificant to be judged against your inner knowing. From a simple decision like getting up in the morning, to the most complex like choosing a life path, the Craft teaches one to identify the knowing/energy that comes from the spark of the Goddess within and to move in accordance with that knowing. This recognition of the Goddess in everything and in every action is what creates the emphasis on individual choice in Wicca.

In the thealogy of feminist Wicca, personal choice based on an internal identification of individual knowledge is the preferred method for deciding on actions. The basis for this belief rests on the premise that if all persons were connected to their lifeforce/Goddess energy, listened to the information gained from this source, and moved at all times in accord with their knowing, they would become self-governing. There would be no need for laws imposed from without. The laws within would create a deeper understanding of the welfare of others and a personal integrity that legislation cannot. In this belief system, moving against what one "knows" creates its own judgement. True dissatisfaction with oneself comes not from failing to meet an externally imposed societal standard, but from choosing to take an action that is contrary to what one "knows" to be correct. Choosing inaction when action is dictated by a knowing can bring equal personal dissatisfaction. If this personal governance is in place, there is no need for an external judge. If one moves with their knowing/energy, there is seldom regret, and there is always a sense of having moved in good faith. Even if the results were not what you expected, if you moved in good faith with your knowing, the action or decision then carried with it the ancient concept of the I-Ching: "no blame."

This belief results in very individualized behavior and decisions by those practicing the Craft. It means that two individuals, faced with exactly the same choice, can make opposite decisions and both be right. For example, two women become pregnant. For both of them this creates conflict. Neither was prepared to have a child at this time in her life. They both consider abortion. One, acting in accord with her inner knowing, decides that she wishes to have the child even though the conception was not planned. She "knows" that to have an abortion would be the wrong thing for *her* to do at this time. The other woman, however, after establishing her inner feelings, decides that to bring a child into her present life circumstances would be a mistake. She decides to have an abortion. Both women are right. This approach is very different from the long-standing attempts to impose decisions about childbearing on women from without. In a feminist Wiccan belief system, if individuals are in touch with their own connection to the Goddess, the need for external legislation about abortion would fall away.

It may come as a surprise to some that even with a strong belief in an internal divinity, many women who consider themselves part of women's religion, do not believe in an actual Goddess. The traditional definition of a deity as an individual with a separate personality and consciousness is not one which is generally accepted. Although there is a lot of talk about the Goddess and some women actually do view her as a personified deity, there is, more often, an acceptance of the Goddess as a symbol of a collective energy source or life force.

The Goddess is often a symbol in women's Wicca and unless one understands that much of the information in Wicca is communicated by symbol, these associations can, at best, be confusing and, at worst, seem ludicrous. For example, one of the primary symbols of the Goddess is the Moon. Let me assure you that no one I know thinks that the Moon is actually the Goddess, only that the attributes of the Moon symbolically reflect those of the Goddess and women. The Moon's three phases, waxing, full, and waning, match the three aspects of the Goddess, maiden, mother, and crone. The twenty-eight day cycle of the Moon matches the menstrual cycle of many women. The way that the Moon reflects light is a symbol for the process of cause and effect in magic (discussed later in this chapter).

If this symbolism is not confusing in and of itself, there are symbols for the symbols. The color silver is a symbol for the light of the Moon, so silver is thought then to be a color associated with the Goddess. The special silver jewelry worn by many Witches is thought to be symbolic of the Moon's light. This means that silver jewelry is a symbol of moonlight, and the Moon is a symbol for the Goddess. This progressive symbolic process can make it difficult to explain to those outside the Craft why certain pieces of jewelry and/or other symbols, or symbols of symbols, may be regarded as tokens of women's association with the Goddess.

The Moon is only one of hundreds of symbols which represent the Goddess in women's spirituality. Women have researched the matriarchy and its symbols, and have also claimed some of the symbols associated with the occult, to develop a long list of symbols (or symbols of symbols) which represent the Goddess. Labryses, snakes, crescent horns, vulvas, eggs, breasts, and pentacles represent only a few of the better known of these associations. Different Goddesses are thought to symbolize different aspects of woman and to provide role models for women that are both traditional and alternative depending on the particular Goddess. In addition to the Moon, other things found in nature are also often considered symbols of the Goddess. Birds, trees, water, rocks, plants, herbs, animals, mountains, fire, even breezes may be associated with the Goddess. This, of course, brings us back to where this discussion of the Goddess started and reinforces that, from a Wiccan thealogical perspective, the Goddess is a part of everything.

■ *Cosmology—The Way It Works*

One of the most common theological discussions thoughout the ages has been the discussion of cosmology. Cosmology is not a word which many of us encounter in our daily activities, so perhaps it would be wise to establish a definition of cosmology before attempting to discuss it. Cosmology is traditionally defined as any theology or philosophy which attempts to explain the nature of the universe. Feminist Witches are currently in the process of creating and remembering a womancentered cosmology. These women are discussing their various perceptions of the universe, how it operates, and their place in it. As one could probably anticipate, any definition of cosmology in women's

Witchcraft is individual. Some women see attempts to define a cosmology as unnecessary, while for others it molds the basis of their magic and as such becomes an area which requires consideration. Within the Affirmation of ♀'s Spirituality there are statements which imply a certain relationship of women and magic to the universe. Considering the meaning of these statements can give insights into the underlying assumptions which constitute a representative cosmology of women's Wicca.

"There Is One Circle of Women's Energy, and I,_____, Am a Part of This Energy and It Is Mine to Direct"

Since the thealogy of women's Wicca holds that there is a spark of divinity in everything, your connection to the Goddess or life force energy lies within you, because you are a part of it. In most cosmologies there is a concept of where in the universe a deity resides and the relationship of that deity to an individual in that universe. In many traditional religions, there exists a concept of the deity being outside of the individual. A deity which is thought to be external is considered a transcendent deity. The concept of the Goddess within is a concept of an incarnate deity or a deity that exists inside the individual.

The concept of the Goddess as an incarnate deity is the premise in The Affirmation on which magic is based. The cosmology of women's Wicca holds that the power which is required to do magic comes from one's connection to the Goddess. Many traditional religions assume that creative power (like their deity) lies outside the individual. Therefore, one must beg or bargain with a deity in order to improve the forms and circumstances of one's life. This approach to a deity is called supplication and can be found in many a Sunday service. "Have pity on me, Oh Lord, my God, a miserable sinner who is not worthy. . . " Many of us raised in traditional organized religion will no doubt recognize this type of statement and will probably be able to think of others that are similar. In the church which I attended as a child, there was a special part of the service dedicated each week to supplicating oneself before approaching the deity through the middleman minister.

Wiccans take a very different approach. The basis of most women's magic and ritual lies in identifying, affirming, and connecting with the Goddess in yourself, and through this connection accessing a collective goddess energy. Since the Goddess is inside each of us, there is no need to beg or bargain with an external deity. As opposed to being the victim of the capricious whims of a deity with which one has little personal contact, any power needed is consistently within reach because you are "a part of this energy and it is yours to direct." In the emerging cosmology of women's Wicca, power is thought to be available to an individual because the Goddess is an intimate part of each woman. This cosmology includes a belief that the power to create and/or change the forms and circumstances of one's life comes from this connection. In order to access this power, one must first affirm one's connection to the Goddess energy and acknowledge one's ability to use this energy to create the desired results in one's life. The abliity to do magic and create change comes from this affirmation. This approach to a deity is called affirmation, and it is a basic tenet of Wiccan cosmology.

"To Take Responsibility for Myself and My Actions and Know That Consciously or Unconsciously, I Have Drawn Situations to Me"

In the cosmology of many traditional religions, one has no part in determining what will constitute the events and actions of one's life. There is instead a belief that god determines the actions, events, and, even in some cases, one's participation in and reaction to the circumstances that form one's life. Different theological interpretations of this belief are the basis for the differences between some of the denominations in Christianity. In some denominations there is a concept of free will, while in others there is a concept of predestination. In free will theology, god just sets things in motion, and then he puts people in their places. Whatever happens is up to the individuals given the forms and circumstances of their lives that he has created. He makes the major decisions, like where you will be born, who your parents will be, what physical attributes you will have, and then he sets you down on the earth plane to fend for yourself within the system that he has made. This, however, conflicts with the idea that god is omnipotent or all-knowing. The theology of an omnipotent god holds that god not only created the forms and circumstances which comprise your life, but he already knows how you will respond to them. In this theory, since god already knows how you are going to act, you really are predestined. In other words, you have no choice but to act in the ways in which god knows you will act. This theology leads to the belief of some denominations that their god already knows who will be saved, and the rest of us will literally go to hell.

The thealogy of women's Wicca posits quite a different theory: a belief that one can create one's life, from begining to end. With this creative power and our connection to the Goddess comes responsibility. If one can create the forms and circumstances of one's life, then one has a responsibilty to take an active part in doing so. In Wiccan cosmology, there is a belief that the life one is leading is not random, but is the result of ideas, beliefs, concepts, and attitudes that one holds about the way the universe "is" or "should be." This cosmology holds that the forms and circumstances which comprise one's life are chosen by an individual, consciously or unconsciously. A primary part of the "craft" of Witchcraft involves developing an understanding of what attitudes, actions, and beliefs created and continue to create the circumstances of one's existence, and attempting to bring these creative agents into consciousness so that this energy can be directed and its effects can be evaluated.

The process of consciously directing energy is truly a craft or skill which requires practice, analysis, and comparison. Most people first encountering the Craft are surprised at the concept of the Craft as an art. This occurs even though examples of students of this art abound in books and movies. From Luke Skywalker learning to direct "the force" in *Star Wars* to the Sorcerer's Apprentice in Disney's *Fantasia*, the concept of the Craft requiring practice, study and skill is present.

The conscious choice to direct creative energy is what feminist Witches refer to as magic. The art and practice of magic involves the conscious direction and refinement of the use of the energy which comes from our internal connection to the Goddess. The process of learning to consciously direct energy (create magic) is similar to that of learning to play a musical instrument. There are some individuals who show a natural skill and others who work more diligently to attain the same results. But for each, a certain amount of daily practice is most often the key to acquiring the skill.

Let's examine how this conscious direction of energy might work. An example is the ancient art of alchemy. Alchemy is not often understood as the Craft exercise that it truly was. The alchemist was attempting transformation. It is most often thought that the purpose of this transformation was to change lead into gold in order to gain wealth. Actually the process of alchemy is a symbolic act. This process sought not to change lead into gold as its first objective, but to change the alchemist. The alchemist would combine energy (in the form of elements and chemicals) in a certain manner and watch for the results. These would be noted, and if the desired results were not obtained, a variation would be added. This too would be noted. As changes occurred in the materials with which the alchemist worked, the theory goes, there also occurred changes in the alchemist.

Alchemy is one type of magic, and a similar process can be applied to other, less tangible, substances. When doing personal magic, one first establishes a "knowing" and translates it into a goal or objective. Then one consciously directs energy toward creating or drawing into one's life the right conditions to achieve this goal, or even realizing the goal itself. The way the energy is directed is specific, and it is noted. The way the energy manifests as the forms and circumstances of one's life is monitored. If the results are not what was intended, the process is repeated and refined until one is able to consistently send out a certain type of energy and receive a specific result. This is the basis of the true Craft of the Wise, or Witchcraft. There are ethical considerations when directing energy in this way which are discussed later.

To take no part in structuring the circumstances of one's life does not simply mean that one is relieved of responsibility. In Wiccan thealogy, the responsibility still rests with the individual regardless of whether the forms and circumstances of her life were generated consciously or unconsciously. Choosing not to pattern the energy which forms one's life is also a choice, and one is equally responsible as if one had consciously directed the energy. If one's creative energy is not directed consciously, it will be directed subconsciously.

Recent explorations of the role of the subconscious have made us more aware of its workings. The subconscious often has a different way of approaching problems than does the conscious mind. It uses metaphor, symbolism, and images to convey meaning. The subconscious may attempt to give clues about the process that it is using to direct energy. These clues are often communicated symbolically: needing a break may become a broken arm or leg, a back problem may indicate that one is carrying too much responsibility. Similarly, the subconscious could attempt to communicate through positive action: decisions to value oneself might draw good health, or a feeling of appropriate personal power may produce a better job or relationships.

In feminist Wiccan cosmology, therefore, there is no such thing as an accident. Consciously or unconsciously, we draw situations to us. Accepting responsibility for drawing what is perceived as a difficult life is extremely hard for some women. Acknowledging a choice to come into a society in which women are undervalued and abused may at first seem like a cosmic form of "blaming the victim." Additionally, accepting responsibility for physical, mental, or other limitations may seem like accepting blame or punishment. Based on the concepts taught by our society, accepting responsibility for the forms and circumstances of our lives may trigger an association with an insidious inculcation, a Puritan concept which goes something like this:

> If God loves you he will provide for you. However, if you (or your father) have done something to offend God, then he will punish you. This punishment may have many forms, foremost among them being poverty, physical challenge, poor health, inconsistent relationships, mental problems, or emotional instability.

Now the strange thing about this concept is that very few people will acknowledge that it is or ever has been a part of Christian thought. However, it is plainly evident in the Old Testament (and it played as strong a part in the early Christian religious movements of the Americas as the Puritan work ethic, which is well acknowledged). The lack of acknowledgment of this concept makes it difficult to confront. To come to an understanding of one's responsibility without adding to it blame or judgement requires, for most of us, significant unlearning.

Why does it matter if one accepts responsibility for the forms and circumstances of one's life? The answer to this is so important in Wiccan thealogy, I wish I could make this next line print in flashing lights. *If you have created the forms and circumstances of your life, then you have the ability to change them!* It is important to acknowledge that you have the ability to create the forms and circumstances of your life, or you are accepting that you have no power to change them. If you believe that you have no power, then you are denying that the spark of the Goddess is within you, and this would go against the most basic of Wiccan thought.

"That I Shall Transform All Negative in My Environment"

But what if the forms and circumstances of one's life seem negative? To view an event or circumstance as negative is largely a matter of perspective. Because we have the power to control our environment, we have the power to transform negativity. First, let's classify some negative experiences and then look at why they may appear negative. Many of the conditions that we have been taught to view as negative are natural events of destruction and death. The foremost of these are called "Acts of God" by the insurance industry. This first type of negative event may be fire, tornado, flood, or other natural disasters. The death of a loved one or friend may also fall into this first category. A second category of negative experiences is those forms or circumstances which are personally challenging. These are life conditions that push us to and often beyond the limits that we have set. The third category, personally disappointing experiences, may cause one to examine her expectations for the persons in and the circumstances of her life. Let's further define some of these negative experiences and explore some strategies to transform them.

The first category, the "Acts of God" experiences, includes what are viewed in Wiccan thealogy as actions of the Crone or the Kali. The idea of positive destruction is so foreign to our culture that some really active unlearning is often required to undertand this concept. The Crone has her time and place as do the Maiden and the Mother. To have too much of what we have been taught to view as positive (the Maiden and Mother energy) would put the world system out of balance. Existence without the Crone would be similar to a city with no garbage collection. Without the Crone the world would be overrun with people, people in pain would live without release, trees would lay where they fell, and no natural cycle of death and rebirth would be possible. I do not intend, at all, to make light of the tragedy of these events, and yet we have all known people to whom death has come as a blessing. The ancient concept of the Crone, the Kali, is one with which our society struggles. We have moved far away from the concepts of timely and appropriate death and the need for cosmic housecleaning. It is difficult for many of us to accept the Kali in ourselves; to accept that "life forms cannot exist without destroying other life forms."[1] We no longer have a concept of appropriate destruction—be that the Crone, the Kali, or the Furies (the Greek Crone Goddesses who punished crimes against women). There are no gentle priestesses to soothe and accept the souls of the dying. Yet the opportunity to transform our perception of these events as negative exists. If one can step outside the compelling societally-imposed grief process taught as a response to these events, they assume a different significance. They can become part of the turning of the wheel, part of the cycle of birth, growth, death, and rebirth, part of a cosmic ebb and flow, part of the transitions which comprise all life. To celebrate even death as a part of the cycle of life is not out of the realm of possibility within Wicca.

The second category of experiences that is most often viewed as negative is those that are personally challenging. This can include physical challenge, learning disabilities, mental problems, health issues, rape, abuse, poverty, and other catastrophic and oppressive circumstances in a woman's life. On the surface there is no doubt that these events appear negative, yet many of the women who have experienced these challenges in their lives have come to view them as situations from which they have learned lessons, and not all negative lessons. They often consider these events formative experiences which made them strong, insightful, or purposefully angry. The fact that these experiences can be viewed as lessons is in no way meant to negate their original anguish or pain, nor does it in any way condone inaction or imply that women should accept circumstances that are oppressive.

I have found this concept to be one of the most difficult cultural attitudes to unlearn, so perhaps an example would be helpful. Although there are probably examples that would be more compelling, I am most comfortable speaking from personal experience, so I share with you some of my challenges. I am dyslexic. For those of you who don't know what that means, I'll try to explain. Dyslexics have a different mode of perceiving the world and although no dyslexics have exactly the same limitations/gifts, many are limited in their ability to order and place a value on written symbols. We are what is termed learning disabled by the scholastic community.

As a child I could not read. I don't mean I wouldn't read; I mean I couldn't read. In addition, my motor coordination was impaired (I couldn't catch, play ball, or dance); I couldn't retain sequential order (like multiplication tables, so I couldn't do math, or letters, so I couldn't spell); I could tell left from right with about a fifteen-second delay (very embarrassing when trying to give directions), and the mysteries of which way a screw or jar lid turns still elude me.

This was devastating to my self-esteem as a child. My teachers thought I was smart but lazy. My classmates thought I was dumb, and they told me so. I really was one of those kids who was picked last in kickball. By the time I was nine I learned to read, but I was personally convinced by my friends, teachers, and the system that I was stupid. I continued for years to have a poor attitude about myself despite the fact that I completed high school, finished college, and began working in jobs that required complex skills. Gradually, I began to notice attributes that I had which were positive as a result of this gift/problem. Because I couldn't write things down, I developed a wonderful memory. I could remember practically anything that I encountered except sequential numbers or letters. Meetings, conversations, books, songs, poems all stayed with me while my friends forgot. Because it was my primary form of communication, my verbal ability soared. Words, concepts and ideas flowed easily. I was differently socialized because I hadn't been able to read. The ideas and images of mainstream culture hidden in the myths and fables used to educate young children were not in my information store. My psychic sense was heightened—I used it more to "pass" as average. Information that other children gained through traditional sources, I gained by employing psychic skills and deductive reasoning. I learned to value equally input from both rational and intuitive sources.

It wasn't until I began to understand the Craft, and through it see the positive effects that this experience had had on my life, that I came to terms with the pain that it had caused me. I began to see how these events that were devastating to me as a child had caused me to develop different attributes that my friends, my community and I valued. I'm now glad that I wasn't able to read until I was older and could be more discerning. It meant that I had less to unlearn. I'm delighted (most of the time) by my heightened psychic abilities. My ability to listen, conceptualize, and articulate concepts seems a rare gift. Finally, the ability to value both rational and intuitive information is an ability that I wouldn't trade (especially for the ability to tell right from left). So what appeared to be a handicap as a child (and still provides some challenges as an adult) has become a very positive thing. I have transformed my attitude and consider myself gifted in a particular way that is different from most. The negativity and pain of my childhood still condition my perceptions, it is true, but in general, I cannot help but feel my life has been enriched because of these challenges.

I could not hope, nor do I intend, to speak for every woman who has experienced personal challenges. I only speak for myself and those women who have shared their challenges with me. For myself and for many of them, I can say that often the events/circumstances that we originally viewed as negative were actually learning experiences and/or power enhancers. These events/circumstances appeared negative, but when all of the ramifications of these experiences came into play, it seemed that it may be have been these very experiences which made us strong and assisted us to identify our personal power and connection to Goddess energy. This is not to say that it didn't hurt. It's just to say that we generated in our life, consciously or unconsciously, the actions and activities which we needed for growth.

The third category of experiences that often seem negative are those which bring personal disappointment: losing lovers/friends, not achieving personal goals, being unable to secure what is perceived to be needed in terms of housing, employment, security, or material possessions. The ability to transform these experiences comes in large part through our ability to transform our expectations and desires. In truth, it is not often these external trappings that make a person happy. Happiness is generated internally, and in many cases it has nothing to do with external circumstances. "The charge of the Goddess," a statement of unknown origin used by Witches to invoke the Goddess in ritual (this particular version was adapted by Starhawk and appears in *The Spiral Dance*), says:

"And you who seek to know Me, know that your seeking and yearning will avail you not, unless you know the Mystery: for if that which you seek, you find not within yourself, you will never find without. For behold, I have been with you from the beginning, and am that which is attained at the end of desire."[2]

For me, this statement refers, in part, to this third category of "negative" experiences. The ability to transform the negativity which accompanies these personally disappointing experiences is an inside job. Demanding that people (including yourself) or events conform to a certain prescriptive formula for your happiness is most often a sure method of creating disappointment and unhappiness. The ability to transform these experiences comes from discerning what are the preferences that one has in regard to a situation, but being able to accept whatever the actual situation is.

Reprogramming negativity is an action which takes place in the head and in the heart. This transformation at times takes place internally through a change in attitude, and at times takes place externally through a conscious action or decision. The transforming of negativity does not condone or imply a Pollyanna attitude. It can and should come from a rational base in addition to an intuitive base. Denial is not a method of transformation. It is a method of avoidance. Transformation that is effective, of necessity, includes acceptance of the situation.

The process of transformation is not a passive one, but an active one. If one is attempting to transform negativity, how would one go about it? There are many possible avenues to follow when deciding what action is appropriate for reprogramming negativity. It is not possible to discuss here all the available options, but what follows is one method which many women have found effective. This particular process for dealing with negative experiences has three steps.

The first step is to identify the problem. At times this is, of course, obvious. At other times, there may be only a vague feeling of uneasiness, discomfort or apprehension. When these unidentified feelings also cause a feeling of negativity, it may be helpful to ask oneself questions like: When did I first start to feel uncomfortable? What about this situation makes me uneasy? What parts of my body feel "funny"? What images are lingering in my mind that upset me? It is extremely difficult to resolve an issue if one is unaware or uncertain of its cause(s). At times, just knowing what caused the feeling of uneasiness is enough to resolve it. If this is true, then the process can stop here.

If knowledge of what is causing feelings of negativity does nothing to relieve the uneasiness, then the second step is to evaluate the problem. This is most useful when it is done both rationally and intuitively. Because of the emphasis our culture places on rational thinking, we may have difficulty accessing, or have a tendency to dismiss, information gained from an intuitive or "feeling" base. It is of equal importance to validate and evaluate how one feels about the issue and how one thinks about it. For example, rationally knowing that there is nothing to fear from a cockroach does not mean that one suddenly becomes comfortable with them. However, approaching the problem intuitively may give one the needed insight to proceed with transforming this fear. It is often helpful when evaluating an issue to create and answer questions for yourself about the situation. Why does this particular situation bother me? Are my expectations about how something "should be" causing me to react negatively? Is this a situation in which I have been culturally conditioned to expect a certain outcome? These and any other questions which seem appropriate can be asked to assist you to evaluate your reaction to the experience. There are basically two possible outcomes of this evaluation process. One either decides the situation is serious, or one decides it is not.

In step three the process branches out in two fairly divergent directions, both of which are possibilities. Step three leads to action or acceptance, depending on the result of the evaluation. If an evaluation of the issue leads one to feel that it is of little concern or significance, then let it go. This act of acceptance is most successful when it is complete, and one accepts all of the issues and concerns around the situation— no more worrying, no more anger, no more frustration, no more fear, no more feeling sorry for yourself, and no more energy spent on the issue.

If, however, you evaluate the problem and feel that it does require attention, or if attempts at acceptance fail, then it is time for action. If action is indicated then asking questions which assist in determining what type of action is possible, required, and/or desired may be helpful. What can be done to change the situation? What risks am I willing to take to move toward resolution? Have I been limiting the possible responses that I have to the situation? Can everyone in the situation win?

Here's an example of how this process might work. "Nancy" has a job which she feels is awful. After coming home from work each day, she feels exhausted, but she's not quite sure why. Her first step is to analyze why her job seems so draining. She seeks a "knowing," and she asks herself questions about her work environment and her co-workers. From this she discovers that she feels pressure from her co-workers not to excel on her job. Now, with this knowledge, she evaluates her situation. She has two basic choices. She can continue to do her work well and accept that this may make some of her co-workers unhappy with her. If Nancy decides that she wishes to pursue this option, she can remain open to her co-workers, but not allow their expectations to define her job for her. The other possibility for Nancy is to decide that she can't continue to work in an environment where she feels so uncomfortable. Many solutions then become possible for Nancy. She can confront her co-workers about their expectations of her. She can go to management and explain the situation. She can attempt to create a different atmosphere which is not competitive. She can look for a new job. She can change her expectations about what approval needs she has from her co-workers or any of the myriad other possible action steps that exist. Nancy is now equipped with information and options which allow her to have control of her situation, and she can direct her energy in ways which allow her to resolve the issue and/or accept it. Nancy has transformed a negative situation.

A problem arises in this process when women reach the decision that a situation is unacceptable and yet are unwilling to take action. To remain in such a situation after establishing a "knowing" which indicates alternative action is necessary means that one is working at cross purposes to one's own energy. Choosing inaction without true acceptance can cause one to feel stuck, trapped, or sick, and may eventually deplete one's personal reserves. To continue in such a situation may actually be hazardous to one's health. In Wiccan cosmology, your connection to the Goddess gives you power and the ability to change the forms and circumstances of your life, and this includes changing your limitations and challenges. This process of transformation of negativity is not limited—there are an infinite number of ways which we can vary the energy we are mixing to create the forms and circumstances of our lives. This transformation of negativity is a reflection of the cycle of birth, death and rebirth. It is the rebirth of hope.

"There Are an Infinite Number of Possibilities for My Life"

When we are young children we believe that anything is possible. When we close our eyes, we disappear. We see creatures and friends that others do not. We fly out windows and return unharmed. We hear and speak with beings who are not physically present and experience any number of other "strange and unusual fantasies" which are the province of childhood. In our society, if we choose to share these experiences with adults they are usually acknowledged in a patronizing way, if at all. It does not take most children long to identify that sharing such experiences does not gain them approval and that experiences of this sort are not considered a part of "reality" in our culture.

Probably the first persons to assist us in establishing our reality are our parents. They condition us to respond to our environment in certain cultural patterns. They assist us to define what is reality and what is not according to what they perceive reality to be. Now it is clear that this is not an entirely negative process; however, it is a limiting process. Children are enculturated to believe that certain things are possible and that others are not. Thus begins a process of perceived limitations to certain life options which may or may not be valid.

The outcome of this process of defining reality becomes particularly clear when one compares the effect that alternate socialization has on children. Children raised in cultures where reincarnation is a part of the belief system remember and discuss it. Past lives are an accepted part of reality in these cultures, so children learn that sharing knowledge and information gained from a past life does not meet with societal disapproval. Children raised in many Native American cultures are taught to acknowledge the voices in the wind and the spirits in the trees. Members of the community who are not able to identify and converse with their spirit helpers are thought to be somewhat impaired, and it may be a cause for pity. Children raised in some fundamentalist Christian churches accept people speaking in tongues. There are any number of "exceptions" to reality, depending on the societal perspective of the individual observing them.

Overall, these definitions of reality serve a positive function which gives children access to a store of knowledge from the other individuals in their culture, both past and present. This process of enculturation causes difficulties, however, when a societal perception of what consititutes reality is skewed and/or limited. Gross definitions of reality often form the boundaries of life experience. These gross definitions allow children to live to adulthood in relative safety and provide a structure for interacting with their environment. Information like, "Bees may sting; fire may burn; and some animals may consider humans tasty," is useful. It is when these definitions become societal absolutes that limitations result. Bees always sting. Fire always burns. Certain animals always eat humans. This allows behavior concerning these things to become prescriptive. Bees and certain animals invoke a fear response and can, therefore, be killed with impunity. Fire must be used and handled only under certain conditions. When learned in childhood and reinforced by one's community, these prescriptive behaviors are most difficult to unlearn and may be so ingrained in an individual that they are not challenged.

Further, over time, these absolute definitions may also begin to govern minor nuances of reality. These definitions may interpret the way people are expected to interact with each other, the way they are to interact with the environment, the way they should appear or be clothed, the way that they speak, or even the way they interact sexually. The possibilities for life can become extremely limited. The societal message is: "If you are _____, then you can't be _____." If you are an artist, then you can't hold a regular job, and you will probably be poor. If you are a good mother, then you can't have a career. If you are a moral person, then you can't expect to be wealthy. If you want to have a good relationship, then you must be willing to sacrifice. Thousands of such messages are carried by each person and pattern their perceptions of reality. In the cosmology of women Wiccans, however, these prescriptive definitions only become true, they are not inherently true.

Why is it that Wiccan cosmology holds that these prescriptive definitions are not necessarily true, but come true? The underlying assumption goes back to the belief that because you are a manifestation of the

Goddess, you have power, and that consciously or unconsciously you are creating your life. The primary manner of creating reality/life is based on what one believes about it, what one expects from it, and what one accepts to be true. This means that the beliefs, ideas, thoughts, words, attitudes, concepts, visions, limitations, and definitions which one accepts about the way life *is* cause life to be the way that one expects it to be. In other words, reality manifests in accordance with our beliefs about what reality is. For many, in fact probably most people, this process is unconscious, so the forms and circumstances that comprise their lives may appear capricious because they are not created consciously.

The premise active in the cosmology of women Witches is that the only limitations which a person has are those which they accept. *All* manner of form is flexible. The way that we perceive the world and the limitations which exist in our lives are the ones which *we* have decided are functioning. These limitations can be those that we have been conditioned to accept by our society or they can be those that we have accepted as individuals. Attempting to unlearn the personal or cultural conditioning that one has adopted about the way things "are" can be truly challenging. For some women this broadening of perspective can even be frightening. It is comforting to think that one knows how the world is structured and that it will respond in certain predictable patterns. When these limitations are removed, the idea that anything can happen may at first seem overwhelming. Simple decisions take on a new perspective as it becomes clear that from each of these decisions, one's life may branch out in different directions.

One way of envisioning unlimited possibilities can be described like this: You are standing at a crossroad. The roads which you may take from this point branch out in many directions or may even go back in the direction from which you came. You may recognize that some of these choices are definitely not options which should be considered. However, some others look to be likely choices. Some of these roads are well worn from others who are on similar journeys and may seem attractive, while some of the roads are overgrown with brush and may appear almost impassable. A life is built as each decision about which road to take leads you to another crossroad or even back to the same one again. There is never only one road. There is never only one way. There is, at every junction, an unlimited number of possible ways which you can proceed.

Witches of the past were often persecuted because they did not accept or follow the societal norm. These women believed that truly any number of things were possible, and because of this belief anything became possible. Psychic communication, healing, magic, contact with non-form beings, and knowledge of the future became things that were part of their reality and a part of their lives because they believed them to be. These are not vestiges of a bygone day to which modern Witches have no access. If you wish for psychic communication, do not attempt it from the perspective of one who is "just testing it out" to see if it is real. The first step is to unlearn any message which says that it isn't. Effective psychic communication comes from a perspective which acknowledges that it is real. With this change of perspective, psychic communication becomes a possibility.

There are certain actions in our culture which are strongly identified with a negative outcome. Freeing oneself from an expectation of negativity in a specific situation may allow one to envision a positive outcome. This outcome may not have been conceivable when viewed according to what we have been culturally conditioned to accept as reality. It is possible that everyone in a situation can win, no matter how much baggage we carry to the contrary. Remember, reality manifests in accordance with our beliefs. Shifting one's beliefs about reality can bring one to a place where there is an unlimited number of possible outcomes to a situation and there is a limitless number of directions for life.

"That I Can Create My Own Reality, and That Sending Out a Positive Expectation Will Bring a Positive Result"

Let's suppose that you are considering going on a trip. You call a travel agent to assist you in making plans for your trip. The travel agent tells you that she will be glad to help you in arranging the trip but that after the trip is underway you cannot make any changes at all regardless of what circumstances befall you. An itinerary for each day will be determined. Where you will stay and even where and what you will eat is all preset. Would you agree to go? Now let's suppose that the trip is to the earth plane. You are choosing to incarnate at a certain time and in a certain place, but you will have no ability to influence further the circumstances of your life. Would you agree to go?

To come to the earth plane with no control over the circumstances of our lives after we get here is not a concept which is supported in feminist cosmology. There is instead the belief that we agree to come here with the ability to order our lives. It seems, however, that often, either

in the transition to form or later, as a result of socialization, we forget
the nature of the mechanism for ordering our lives. Fortunately, some
people either don't forget, have some alternative experience (vision
quests, drugs, a life-after-death experience), or simply progress to the
point where they remember the mechanism for order. It is interesting
to note that in almost all spiritual traditions these mechanisms are similar. What it is called and how it works are often different, but it seems
that some procedure for ordering one's life exists in virtually every tradition. In general, it is a way of stating to the cosmos/deity what it is
that one would like to have happen. It can be what is commonly called
prayer, contemplation, directing energy, visualization, and in some
cases, meditation.

In the cosmology of women's Wicca this process of ordering one's
life is considered an active process, as differentiated from the passive
process of supplicative prayer, contemplation, or meditation. This active process of visualization and channeling energy is not the province
of women's spirituality alone but is present in almost all metaphysical
traditions, both ancient and New Age. The ability to channel/direct energy in the Craft, as mentioned earlier, is what is called magic. It is the
way that most Witches believe we order our lives.

Before attempting to explain women's magic, it is important to establish a common context for some of the terms used. Most magic starts
by acknowledging the world of form. It is easy to recognize the world
of form because it is what our society has taught us is valid and accepted as reality. The world of form consists of the seemingly solid
things which comprise acknowledged existence. Next, in women's
cosmology, there is the "less-commonly-perceived realm." This is the
portion of the universe which is generally not acknowledged by our
society. It is thought, by most feminst Witches, to comprise energies
which are not manifest in form but which, nevertheless, exist. It is
the less-commonly-perceived realm which is hostess to disincarnate
individuals, psychic energy, spirits, elementals, auras, plant divas,
and many more such energies. In some systems, the less-commonly-
perceived realm is referred to as the "astral" plane, but this has become
a loaded word and is not often used in feminist Craft. Still others call it
the invisible realm, which was a term I used until someone pointed out
to me that for many people it is not invisible.

With this knowledge of the components of the Wiccan cosmos, let's
proceed on to how the process of structuring reality (creating order) is
thought to work. First, simply stated, the working equation which is

believed by most women Witches to be functioning goes like this: A person holds a certain belief. They take certain actions based on this belief. The belief itself and the actions taken based on the belief generate energy. This energy patterns what is possible in her world. It forms the substance of the less commonly perceived realm. This patterned energy carries over from the less-commonly-perceived realm into the world of form and continues to create reality in accordance with the original belief.

In other words, the less-commonly-perceived realm is the place of formation, and the world of form is the place of manifestation. The attitudes which we collectively hold about the way the world "is" blend together to create the universe that we live in and the lives that we lead. Each individual creates a portion of the world of form, and together we all create what is perceived to be reality. These attitudes form the substance of our existence by influencing the less-commonly-perceived realm. In Wiccan cosmology, many believe there is a substance of which all things are formed. This substance is believed to exist in both the world of form and the less-commonly-perceived realm. In ancient Craft traditions, this substance was called ether. Ether was considered to be the basic matter of all creation. There are women in women's spirituality who hold a concept similar to that of ether. There are others who, although they believe they can influence some cosmic force, either choose not to name it at all or name it Goddess. Attitudes and actions in the world of form mold ether. The energy created by these attitudes and actions forms the ether of the less-commmonly-perceived realm and then manifests in the world of form as the circumstances of one's life. We have created "reality."

So in the cosmology of women's Wicca, if one wishes to create positive events and circumstances in one's life, one has the power and ability to do so. By evaluating and examining the attitudes which one holds about the way the world "is" and by replacing any which one finds to be unacceptable, one generates new beliefs. These new beliefs then re-form reality. In this equation, it is presumed that positive beliefs create positive results. In women's Wicca, then, the method of ordering reality is through consciously directing the energy which forms one's life through magic. This process can wear many names: spells, words of power, ritual, directing energy, and even psycho-therapy can all be ways in which women take charge of their beliefs. Although there are many different names for this process and many different ways to accomplish an objective, in women's thealogy choosing to take charge of the energy which patterns one's existence is basic.

An excellent explanation of bringing this process into conscious awareness is given by Marion Weinstein in her book *Positive Magic: Occult Self Help*. Weinstein calls the process of consciously directing energy "Words of Power:"

> "Come to me for my speech hath power to protect, and it possesseth life. . . .for I am Isis the goddess, and I am the lady of words of power, and I know how to work with words of power, and most mighty are (my) words."[3]

Positive Magic is the best existing book for learning the techniques of directing positive energy. Although this book is not written exclusively from a woman-centered spiritual perspective, it is, nevertheless, an excellent step-by-step guide to creating a positive reality.

"That I Shall Grow to Understand the Cyclic, Life Affirming, Rhythms of the Earth, and Always Act With Love Toward Her and All Her Plants and Creatures"

One can't proceed very far in women's spirituality without noticing the emphasis on cycles. There are the cycles of the seasons, the changes of which are celebrated as holidays in women's spirituality. There are the cycles of women themselves: through life as the Maiden, Mother, and Crone, and through the month as menstruating women ebb and flow. There are the cycles of birth, life, and death, or generation, decay, and regeneration, that exist in all life. There are the natural cycles of the food chain, the rain cycle, the cyclic response of plants to the seasons, the cycles of migrating birds, cycles of hibernation in some animals, the cycles of the Moon, and the resulting cycles of the oceans and tides.

Each of these cycles, and the hundreds of others that exist, can be considered part of a blueprint: a clue we have given ourselves to indicate the way in which the universe is intended to operate. It is one of the highest goals in women's Wicca to be able to recognize the patterns of these cycles and to move in accord with the energy generated by them. The natural cycles of the earth and her plants and creatures provide examples to the observant of successful ways to interact with the cycles of the earth. These cycles are not only observed but often imitated by the rituals and spells of women's magic.

Women's Wicca is primarily a nature religion. This may be a distancing statement for some women. Those of us who have studied sociology or mainstream theology may have been taught to hear "nature religion" as a slur. In traditional sociology and theology, the term most often equates to a primitive form of religious expression. It indicates that the adherents of a "nature religion" are simplistic in their religious analysis and have not taken their religious interpretations beyond the most basic definitions. To feel positive about being part of a nature religion often requires that one approach it from a different perspective.

In our culture from the time that we are children most of us are taught to distance ourselves from nature and to perfunctorily perform almost daily actions which by their very nature, remove us from the natural cycles of the earth. The pace and attitudes of mechanized society do not acknowledge or promote a connection to nature. Electric lights distort the daily cycle of light/dark, calendars ignore the cycles of the Moon, emphasis on indoor activities removes us from seasonal changes, and denial of astrological influences wipes out any connection to even the gross cycles of the planets. Women are taught to hide their cycles and act at all times as if they feel the same. Young women are taught to act older, old women are told to act younger. And all of these elements are forged into a linear time frame which is difficult not to honor. In addition, for many women who live in an urban environment, a world of asphalt and activity exclude them from any semblance of the natural universe.

In the cosmology of women's Wicca, however, there is a strong emphasis on our connection to nature. For many women it is through a connection to the natural world and natural cycles that intuitive "knowings" emerge. Contact with nature and honoring natural cycles bring knowledge of the self and knowledge of Goddess energy. Celebrations of cycles in Wicca are the "markers" that women use to remind themselves of changing earth energies. Astrology is viewed by many as a science of anticipating the effects of cycles. Women's Witchcraft does not honor a linear time frame, but affirms the cyclic nature of women's lives as part of the natural universe. The direction of mechanized society and traditional religion away from nature is considered by many women Witches to be one of the prime reasons for the current exploitation of the Earth. There is a hope that if people understood the various cycles of the Earth and nature they would choose not to act in an exploitative way.

In the same way that Witches believe that there is a spark of the Goddess/lifeforce energy in each individual, there is a belief that this spark also resides in each individualization of creation. The idea that the

Goddess/lifeforce energy lives in all natural things is accepted by most women Wiccans. Therefore, to show disrespect to any natural thing or to use it in an exploitative way is to exploit the Goddess energy both in the thing and, because you are a part of the same energy, in your self. Actions which are intentionally destructive move against the Goddess and cause a distancing from her. To perform any action which is, by nature, negative and/or which goes against one's knowing requires that one distance one's self from her own Goddess energy.

This acceptance of the Goddess/lifeforce energy in every aspect of creation and the emphasis in women's religion on cycles are what cause it to be identified as life affirming. This identification, it seems, may at times be a response to the perceived linear death orientation of traditional religions. In many traditional religions, the resurrection of the god is overshadowed by what may appear to be the worship of his death. The concept of worshipping a dying god, who is observed to have little continuing relationship with his creation, is viewed by some women as a death cult. In addition, the emphasis in some traditional religions on a single life existence is believed to be linear, unlike the cyclic reincarnation thealogy of women's Wicca.

How is it that women honor the earth? For each woman this is individual. Many women live close to the earth and try to live in ways which are in harmony with the environment. Others may be strongly involved in ecological activism or quietly composting for their backyard gardens. Another woman may choose to be a vegetarian, while still another may recycle everything from envelopes to glass jars. Another woman may organize rituals for healing the earth where she and other women can direct energy for protecting the planet. While still another woman may stand alone in front of her altar and light a simple candle. In the way of Wicca, each woman is encouraged to look to her inner knowings and find her own way to honor the planet which is her creation.

"That My Only Power Is In the Present"

The cyclic conception of women's Wicca challenges the way we have been taught to view time. We have been taught that time is something that can be borrowed, wasted, used, spent, and squandered. We have been educated to view the progress of "man" as being linear. In this concept, men (with women being literally dragged along) have progressed from savagery to today's technology. Occasionally examples of backsliding (like the Dark Ages) are cited, but primarily we are educated to believe that this progress has been ever forward. Examples of linear thinking abound, from the structured use of measured time to the burying of nuclear waste. Linear thinking even surfaces in some religions which have a concept of reincarnation. In these, a soul progresses through time, beginning at the dawn of time (only in a linear frame could time dawn) as a flea and gradually, life by life, becoming more advanced as the world also grows older.

In the cosmology of women's Wicca, these concepts of progressive linear time are regarded by most as limiting. The emphasis on cycles in feminist cosmology brings with it a different view of time. This concept is articulated in the saying, "All time is now." This implies that time, as we have been taught to view it, is artificial. There are many different ways in which one can measure time, and each of these conditions to some extent what that culture views as reality. In other words, people are inculturated to view time in certain ways. Studies about time perception in children show that they have difficulty judging time intervals of more than two seconds until they are around seven or eight years old. This seems to indicate that children learn to perceive time from the others around them. Cultures close to nature often measure time from moon to moon. Many begin their year on a different day from most of the Western world. The Pagan year celebrates the cycle of growth, fullness, and decline, while the traditional Gregorian calendar blends religious and politically expedient dates into a calendar which seems to have little relation to anything.

In feminist cosmology the view that all time is now allows for a different perspective. Time is viewed as a voluntary system that one has chosen to participate in while on the earth plane. It is useful and allows events to be perceived in a seeming sequence. We, however, are not locked into perceiving time in this manner. One may, if it is helpful or necessary, step outside the time continuum. An example of this is some forms of divination. Divination which provides information about the future or the past takes place outside the traditional time sequence. The fact that information gained in this way is outside the time continuum may be one reason why our culture has such difficulty accepting it. Interestingly enough, this concept of the eternal present is now postulated by science as a possible theorem growing out of Einstein's relativity theory. So the ancient time concepts postulated by Witches for centuries and the scientific community, surprisingly, are beginning to find themselves in agreement about the nature of time.

Further, in the cosmology of women's Wicca, reincarnation need not be necessarily progressive. If one steps outside the time continuum, then one can choose to reincarnate at any moment in time. The first thing that this statement implies is that reincarnation is a choice. As previously discussed, there is a concept of free will in feminist spiritual cosmology and this extends to the ability to reincarnate as one chooses. Disincarnate beings are thought to reside in the less-commonly-perceived realm, which is outside the time/space continuum. A disincarnate individual is free to consider incarnating at any time according to what is needed by that entity or what the entity wants as the form and circumstances of a life. What this means in practice is that one could choose to incarnate first in 1643 C.E. (Common Era) and then in 24 C.E. and then 1934 C.E. and then 49 B.C.E. (or any other order) if this was the sequence which would provide the most challenge and/or growth potential.

Feminist Witches have taken this view of time very seriously, and this aspect of feminist cosmology forms a basis of thealogy and magic. The ability of an individual to affect the past or the future is considered negligible. It is believed that there is only one "now" moment that all time exists within, therefore, working magic which is to influence either the past or the future is thought to have little effect. In further validation of this concept, spells and words of power are thought to be most effective when stated in the present tense. Statements in words of power like, "I am becoming healthy," preclude the possibility of being healthy in the present and focus on health happening at some future date. When working with the concept that all time is now, one would choose instead to make a statement like "I am healthy," assuming that the only true place of power is in the eternal now moment. Women of spirit continue to refine working outside the accepted timeframe, unlearning linear thoughts which we have been enculturated to perceive, and choosing instead to base our cosmology on an alternative reality that time, like form and space, is flexible.

So feminist Witches' cosmology includes a concept of an incarnate deity, affirmation, no concept of predestination, a concept of personal power, and an identification of the cyclic nature of the universe which includes a concept of the necessary nature of challenge and diversity. It holds a nontraditional perspective on how the world is organized and what ability an individual has to affect change. Wiccan cosmology establishes for its adherents a framework for living and interacting in the world which promotes personal power and gives us power over our lives.

Establishing and being able to articulate a cosmology is by no means a requirement for participation in women's magic or ritual. Many women who have channeled energy both through ritual and spellcraft for years have no working knowledge of any cosmology, only a sense of what works. For other women, however, the cosmology of women's Wicca provides a working model of a universe that affirms women's strength and power while validating an alternate spiritual, ethical, and social structure which is essential in affirming women's experience.

■ Ethics

"That I Shall Try Never to Use My Energy Unwisely or to Limit the Free Will of Another"

"That I Shall Never Use My Energy for What I Know to Be Evil, Aggressive or Manipulative and Shall Only Use My Energy for What I Know to Be Positive Ends"

These two statements in the Affirmation are so closely associated and build on each other in such a way that considering them as a set provides the most clarity. They deal with an emerging ethical structure among spiritual women. There is, in feminist spirituality, a strong sense of ethics. How it manifests itself and what it means is one of the topics which is currently being discussed and defined by women of spirit. At this time there are basically two ethical thealogies operating in the Wiccan women's community. For the purpose of this discussion, I will call these two thealogies the Aradians and the Positive Practitioners. These are not names which are in general use in the women's community, but they are descriptive terms that give information about the thealogical position of each.

Aradians

The beliefs of the Aradians have grown largely out of a seemingly logical extension of the women's movement. The underlying belief, simply stated, is that women as an oppressed group have a special connection to magic and that we have a responsibility to use our power, including our psychic energy and magic, to end our oppression. Although this belief definitely grew out of the politics and philosophy of the women's movement, it is strongly supported by the work of Charles Leland in his book *Aradia: Gospel of the Witches*.* The materials in *Aradia*, Leland claims, were purchased from an Italian Witch and are from her Book of Shadows. There has been much speculation in both Pagan and scholarly circles about the authenticity of Leland's claims, but regardless of this, the book is used by some Aradians to explain and justify their position. The major piece in *Aradia* is a story/myth about the Goddess Diana and her daughter Aradia. In the myth, Diana, troubled by the suffering of the people on earth, sends her daughter Aradia as a teacher. Aradia brings gifts and information which can help all people, but which are particularly designed to assist the oppressed through knowledge and magic.

Aradians, based in part on Leland's work, believe that it is a moral obligation of women to use whatever means necessary to interrupt, intervene, and end the oppression of women. The fact that this may include manipulation, cursing, or hexing of the perceived oppressor is considered just. For some Aradians, manipulative magic is used only against an identified institutional oppressor. For others, however, if a lover (male or female), boss, or friend acts in ways which are disappointing, manipulative magic can also be used to assist these offenders to bring their behavior into alignment with the Aradian's desires.

The Positive Practitioners

Positive Practitioners, on the other hand, believe that there is *never any* reason for negative or manipulative magic. Using oppressive magic to end oppression only puts one in the same position as the oppressor. Their belief is based on three concepts that are basic to a Positive Practitioner's understanding of the Craft: the Wiccan Rede, the three-fold law, and the doctrine of free will.

■ The Rede

Positive Practitioners strictly interpret the Wiccan Rede and the three-fold law. Traditionally stated, the Rede is "And ye harm none, do as thou wilt." This is the only "rule" in Wicca. The Rede is believed by some to be a remnant of ancient Witchcraft which has been passed from one Witch to another through the ages. Others believe that Gerald Gardner, an English Witch who popularized Witchcraft in the 1950s, is responsible for its creation. Regardless of the origin of the

Rede, Positive Practitioners believe that the Rede states the most basic belief of women's Wicca: that one never, under any circumstances, uses energy for actions or activities which are known to be harmful. This is the philosophy which is reflected in the Affirmation of ♀'s Spirituality.

For many women after the "thou shalts" and "thou shalt nots" of traditional religions, the Rede seems, at first to be quite freeing. It is only after attempting to work magic and direct energy within the Rede that most women become aware of the subtle judgement required to identify what constitutes harm. There is no doubt among the Posititve Practitioners that cursing, hexing, and binding constitute harm and, therefore, violate the Rede. They refuse to participate in any action or circle which is intended to limit anyone, regardless of their status as an oppressor.

■ The Three-Fold Law

The willingness of Positive Practitioners not to use their energy to stop perceived oppressive acts is based largely on the three-fold law. The three-fold law, like the Rede, is of uncertain origin. It states that the energy one sends out is returned to the sender three-fold. In other words, the energy which one sends out manifests in one's life. The three-fold law then goes even farther to express an expectation that the energy of these actions will return to an individual three times. This is the basis of the belief in karma in women's Wicca.

Most feminist Witches believe strongly in karma, which can be defined as a system of cosmic balance which brings to each individual the benefits and consequences of her actions. The ethical thealogy of Positive Practitioners is based on the three-fold law as a representative system of karma. Positive Practitioners believe that there is no need to interrupt the actions of an oppressor because the three-fold law will bring back to them exactly what is deserved. To direct energy which limits the free will of anyone would create negative karma for the one directing energy in this way. According to the Positive Practitioners, there is no need to damage one's own karma by limiting the free will of another.

This, however, does not limit Positive Practitioners' political activism. They do participate in marches, political actions, and protest activities. To direct energy which is manipulative is considered to be a violation of the Rede, but to express preferences about the way that one would like life on the earth to be is considered a responsibility.

■ *The Doctrine of Free Will*

The concept of free will was mentioned earlier as a portion of the doctrine of personal responsibility. Basically, it asserts that all individuals have free will, have made choices about what their lives on the earth plane will be, and continue to make choices about how they will live their lives. These choices are not preset but are determined by each person on a case by case basis. The responsibility to act and relate to others in an ethical manner extends to include a respect for the ability of individuals to make their own personal choices. The fact that one can exercise power over another individual or control a situation does not give one the right to manipulate either the situation or the persons involved in it. Positive Practitioners believe that to intentionally interfere in the decisions or actions of another person, no matter how minor that interference might be, constitutes manipulation. Manipulation is considered to be a form of harm and, therefore, in violation of the Rede.

Aradians believe that the three-fold law, the Rede, and the doctrine of free will do not apply to an oppressor; that one's ethics can, and should, be selectively applied. Although many of these women would never consider manipulating a "sister," they would, with very little hesitancy, hex a corporation or a nuclear plant. The Aradians charge the Positive Practitioners with having been seduced by New Age jargon designed to keep the oppressed in their place, while the Positive Practitioners feel that the Aradians are compromising their karma by engaging in manipulative magic. The Positive Practitioners believe that the Aradians hold a simplistic analysis and that they have adopted the the tools of the enemy, while the Aradians feel that the Positive Practitioners are not willing to stand up for the rights of women. There are those who claim that there is a middle path using mild binding spells and not "true manipulative magic," but most Positive Practitioners would say there is no such thing. One is either on a positive path or one is not.

Ideas about ethics are strongly felt. There is no clear way to anticipate which types of women will fall into either of the these two groups. This is probably the topic which is under the most extensive debate at this time in the women's spiritual movement. It remains to be seen if feminist Witches can give each other enough space to hold different ideas and still consider themselves part of one movement or if this issue will cause the first major thealogical split among women of spirit. Obviously, from the statements that this section is based on,

I and the Affirmation of ♀'s Spirituality support the Positive Practitioners.

■ The Blend of Feminism and Spirituality

Several of the concepts found in the Affirmation of ♀'s Spirituality have grown not as much out of the Craft as they have out of the ideas and values of the women's movement itself. This is not to say that these ideas are in conflict with the values expressed in Craft tradition. It is rather that many women involved in women's spirituality have arrived at these values not through a spiritual process alone but also from a political perspective brought to them through the women's movement. They have then translated these concepts into spiritual values. Although traditional or mainstream Wicca is showing more of an understanding and emphasis on political awareness, during the rise of the women's movement, many mainstream covens and Pagan groups held (and some still hold) very conservative concepts of the role of women. Most of the political values in women's spirituality grew, not out of traditional Wicca, but out of an incorporation of feminist ideology into feminist spirituality.

"To Be Myself"

One of the strong values brought to women's spirituality through the women's movement is the value of being one's true self. The conservative view of women often carries with it messages that who we are is not good enough. It implies that in order to be accepted and appreciated as a woman in our culture we must not show our true selves. We are taught that women who are too big, too strong, too outspoken, or too opinionated are not ladylike and must adopt a different demeanor to succeed in relationships or in employment.

During the rise of the women's movement the heavy price of trying to modify one's behavior to "fit" societal standards was often discussed. For many women, this denial was a major source of personal conflict. The essence of this enlightenment translated easily into the beginnings of a spiritual ideology. These concepts became part of women's Wicca with its strong emphasis on self-knowledge, individual definition, and personal choice. Within feminist Craft, the ideal is for each woman to be allowed and encouraged to be herself and never to disguise or compromise what she knows to be true.

"That I Shall, As Much as I Am Aware, Act in Honesty to Myself and to Others"

This same ideology naturally extended into a strong emphasis on honesty both within the women's movement and through it into women's spirituality. Many women had felt forced to lie to each other and even to themselves to be accepted and to succeed. This had effects which were often personally damaging. A lack of personal honesty caused women to be both unaware of and/or unable to state what they experienced as truth. Because of this experience, there emerged within the women's movement a high value on knowing one's self. This value included being able to share what one experienced as truth with others.

This has proved to be one of the most difficult challenges of the women's movement. Women who have been conditioned to hide their true feelings and knowledge have struggled to find a voice. It has generated both a form of brutal honesty and accusations that some women are not open and do not share themselves with others. In the Craft, with its additional value on the appropriateness of silence, many veterans of the women's movement have found the balance and healing that the women's movement alone lacked. Although it is very important to identify and acknowledge what one knows to be true, in the Craft one is not bound to share this information. Choosing to disclose information about oneself or to honestly confront another is considered a positive step, but so is having the wisdom to know when that choice would cause separation and harm.

"To Be Strong and Independent Even in the Midst of Struggle"

Within the women's movement there has been tendency to become frustrated by processes and/or to question the ethics and motives of others. This has sometimes led to the abandonment of both work in process when it became too intense and/or to the inability to associate with friends if they seemed too critical or were discovered to hold different values. Many women wounded in the struggle with sisters have vanished from the movement entirely, while others have sought a framework for their continuing interactions in the thealogy of women's Wicca. Among spiritual women who have remained involved with women's issues an expectation has emerged that one would always try to allow another woman to follow what she knows to be true. This has helped in creating a value in the community of womanspirit of not allowing struggle to separate women who hold different ideologies. The women's spiritual community includes many veterans of the women's movement and also women new to both the women's movement and to the Craft. These women are together seeking a way to include all women.

"To Accept and Understand Those Whose Ethnic or Racial Background, Social or Economic Class, Appearance, or Sexual Preference Are Different from My Own"

The women's movement has held as an ideal the inclusion of *all* women regardless of their background, culture, age, sexual preference, race or differing ability. It has reflected this ideal in many of its activities. There are active anti-racism groups. There have been and continue to be intense discussions about the role that class plays both in personal relationships and in the women's movement at large. The women's movement has been primarily responsible for fat liberation. Accessibility arrangments for differently abled persons are a consideration in almost all event planning. These values have carried over to become part of women's spirituality.

As pointed out earlier in this chapter, the thealogy of women's Wicca includes a concept that each individual is a part of the same Goddess/lifeforce energy. To erect or enforce any barriers between women or to exclude any woman from participation would be to exclude a portion of the Goddess from one's life. A primary goal of spiritual women is the incorporation of every portion of Goddess energy possible into one's life. Intentionally choosing to exclude another woman, based on her appearance, age, sexual preference, differing ability, ethnic or racial background, social or economic class, and to therefore exclude a portion of the Goddess/lifeforce energy, is unthinkable.

"To Stand Firm and Committed to Women and My Spiritual Beliefs Even in Times of Isolation, Pain, Desperation or Negativity"

Women are not immune to questioning their spiritual beliefs in times of personal pain. The loss of a loved one through either death or separation, lack of financial resources, and poor health may cause anyone to wonder if their spiritual ideology holds true. This statement in the Affirmation acknowledges that these times do come, but that there is an intent to remain committed to one's beliefs regardless of life circumstances.

It is often easy to follow a spiritual path if there are no obstacles. It is much more difficult to continue to have a positive perspective during difficult times. Both within the women's community itself and from those on the outside there have been accusations that women's spirituality is a trend; that it is currently "in" in many groups to be "into" women's spirituality. Of course, for some women this may be true, but for many, women's spirituality is a way of life. This means that in good times and bad, women committed to a woman-centered spirituality remain steadfast in their beliefs. In fact, for many women, remembering Wiccan cosmology and thealogy and practicing the Craft during difficult times is a part of the magic of women's spirituality.

■ **Magic and The Craft**

"That Every Situation Is an Opportunity to Practice and Develop My Craft"

There are several statements in the Affirmation of ♀'s Spirituality which deal directly with the concepts of magic and its place in the thealogy of women's Wicca. The concept of magic, or the conscious direction of energy, has often been mentioned throughout this chapter. This is because taking charge of one's life by directing energy is one of the most basic beliefs and skills in the Craft. If we draw situations to us, then what is happening in our lives is no accident. We are drawing to us exactly the persons, experiences, and situations that we need. In the thealogy of feminist Witchcraft, challenges are not things which should be cursed nor looked upon as the whims of capricious fate. Challenges are energy being returned in a different way. This energy recycles to offer an opportunity to devise and perfect the way one's energy is sent out and to judge and refine the result. This process of consciously directing energy is what is called 'magic' in feminist Wiccan cosmology.

Challenges viewed from this perspective are opportunities. Our responses to difficult people at home and at work can be dealt with through the Craft. Lack of personal resources, both financial and emotional, are issues which can be addressed with magic. Viewed from this perspective, a life without challenges could quite possibly be a life which held little chance to develop and perfect one's magic. At times, it may seem that an unchallenging life would be attractive, but a life situation that offers little chance for personal growth is for most women boring and in a cosmic sense is not productive.

When life challenges are viewed as opportunities, magic can become a part of every daily activity. The constant pattern of energy sent and energy returned is considered in every aspect of one's life. Interacting with others, making decisions about how one will behave, what one is willing to do to gain money, dealing with financial and/or health issues, even recycling one's garbage, all become more than simple everyday concerns. They become the way which one can practice directing energy. They provide the stimulus which allows one to refine how one directs energy and often the constant by which one can judge results.

As an example of how this process is considered to work, let's look at the following incident: "Susan" has a lover, "Mare." Mare is bright, intellectually stimulating and enjoys the outdoors. Susan enjoys living with her. She delights in their shared hikes, interesting discussions, and mutual counterculture values. There are, however, problems in their relationship. Mare is not personally responsible. She is at a stage in her life where holding a forty-hour-a-week job is not something that she feels that she can do either personally or politically. Mare refuses to deal with transportation issues even though they live in the country, which puts an additional burden on Susan. Eventually, these and other issues drive them apart. Susan is clear on what she considers to "be wrong" with their relationship, and she decides to use her energy in the form of magic to draw to herself another relationship. This time Susan is very careful to state that she wants a relationship with someone who has a job, a car, and is willing to take responsibility for herself. In no time at all, Susan's new lover appears, and she has all the requirements that Susan stipulated. There is, however, after a short time, another problem. Susan's new lover does not share her interest in nature. Sharing the out-of-doors with this new lover does not seem to be worth all the preparation and hassle that it takes. Attempts to discuss politics, world affairs, or even a good book seem to bore her new lover, and their values seem far apart. Very quickly Susan decides that this relationship is not what she was looking for and leaves her new lover.

These events shared in this way, of course, do not express the amount of personal challenge which was felt by both Susan and her lovers. Susan was drawing to herself the experiences which she needed for several things. This experience made her aware of how extremely literal the result of directed energy can sometimes be. It also pointed out to her that when assessing a situation, it is important not to take things for granted. Further, shared in this way, how Susan's energy manifested becomes obvious. Many times, the way one directs energy is not as obvious as in this example and, in fact, it may not be a conscious decision at all. Also, many times the result is not as obvious either. The ability to analyze and determine what specific action, thought, or belief is causing one's life circumstances to manifest in a certain way is one of the most challenging aspects of women's magic. Learning to control, identify and correlate energy being sent out and the way that energy manifests is a skill which feminist Witches consider to be one of the most basic and yet most challenging aspects of the Craft.

"That I Shall Grow in Wisdom, Strength, Knowledge, and Understanding"

For many women, further development of their Craft is based on their ability to recognize the similarity of events, actions, conflicts, and beliefs that form one's life and to use that knowledge and ability to create the life forms and circumstances which are desired. This skill blends with the strong emphasis on cycles in women's spirituality. The ability to recognize cycles or patterns allows one to respond to one's life and environment with an understanding of how, in the past, energy has manifested. For those who can see the pattern, the effects of practicing the Craft become cumulative. The ability to recognize these recurring patterns and to direct energy in ways which bring a specific result is often considered to be wisdom. If one thinks about the common attributes of an "old wise woman" they are often that she possesses the ability to see and articulate what result commonly follows a certain action and to suggest other possible solutions. It is this ability, along with other strengths, which make her seem wise.

Internalizing the values implied in feminist Witchcraft and attempting to bring them into reality in one's life bring with it wisdom, strength, knowledge and understanding. A knowledge of feminist cosmology brings with it confidence because it outlines a working system in a structured universe. A commitment to accept others who hold different values and attitudes brings with it understanding. Daring to be one's self and to hold to one's spiritual beliefs brings strength.

Many women expect that as they progress toward wisdom, knowledge, and understanding that their lives will become easier. Although for some women this is in fact true, for many more it seems that as one progresses, life does not truly become easier, it becomes more complex. Issues that would at one time have been overwhelming may no longer be troubling, but challenges which require further refinement are presented. As one gains the ability to see the patterns of energy sent, to value intuitive information, to gain the results that one desires, and even during difficult times, to interact in a positive way with one's environment and the people in it, further complexity is welcomed as the next step in one's unfolding journey.

The concepts of women's thealogy are both ancient and brand new. Over the past 15 years during the re-emergence of women's spirituality, women's thealogy has not been far behind, giving women a much needed basis for both personal growth and political work. Although articulations of feminist thealogy are only now emerging and discussion is still very preliminary, there is already the beginning of a dynamic woman-centered cosomology, ethic, and world view which affects each woman who chooses to explore feminist Craft.

A major goal of the women's movement is social change. It has seemed to many of us that positive social change was not possible in any timely way due to the early inculturation of women in a society which taught anti-feminist values to both women and men. The thealogy of women's Wicca is a thealogy of empowerment. It is a strong, individually defined philosophy which provides a basis for women to define for themselves what they view as truth and the means to incorporate these spiritual beliefs into their lives.

■ Resources

Charles G. Leland, *Aradia: Gospel of the Witches*. New York: Samuel Weiser, 1974.

■ Notes

1. Barbara Walker, *The Crone*. San Francisco: Harper & Row, 1985, p. 72.
2. Starhawk, *The Spiral Dance*. San Francisco: Harper & Row, 1979, p. 77.
3. Marion Weinstein, *Positive Magic: Occult Self-Help*. Custer, Washington: Phoenix Publishing Co., 1981, p. 205. Quoted by Weinstein from E.A. Wallis Budge, *The Gods of the Egyptians, Vol. II*. New York: Dover Publications, Inc., p. 207.

CHAPTER 3

Women's
Spirituality
and
Neo-Paganism

The terms used to describe women's spirituality, neo-Paganism, feminist spirituality, and other variations of alternative spiritual traditions often provide little clarity. As they are currently used, any number of meanings can be assigned to a majority of these terms. The women who have come to women's spirituality through the women's movement and those who have come to it through neo-Paganism may fall into more than one category or classification. The following terms and classifications should by no means be thought to constitute the definitive word on either the varieties or the definitions of women's spirituality or neo-Paganism. They can, however, be considered a general guide to the many contexts in which these terms are used.

It is difficult to determine where to begin to describe the relationship between women's spirituality and neo-Paganism. Perhaps the best analogy is that they are two streams flowing into the same river. Although women's spirituality has grown up separately from the Pagan revival, they have both come to similar places, and, in many ways, their philosophies and thealogy/theology, overlap. Often the women's spirituality movement and neo-Paganism parallel each other, while at other times they diverge widely. This chapter attempts to show some of these areas of commonality between women Witches and mainstream Pagans and also areas of difference.

■ Women's Spirituality

In order to clarify women's religion and women's spirituality, it is important to understand the common terms used to discuss and define them. Women all over the globe have been rediscovering and creating an affirming spirituality. Because of the varied backgrounds and geographic locations of these women, the use of different words to describe similar activities and the use of similar words to describe different activities are very common in the community of womanspirit. The women who are practicing women's spirituality are extremely diverse, as are the terms that they use to discuss and describe their spiritual traditions.

Probably the broadest term used by these women is "women's spirituality" which can have many different meanings depending on how it is used and who is using it. "Women's spirituality" is used in this book as an inclusive term to describe traditions inside and outside the feminist movement. It is used both by women who define themselves as Witches and by those who do not. In common usage, it most often refers to any number of progressive philosophies or thealogies that are woman-centered to some degree. It can include neo-Pagan, feminist, Dianic, lesbian, and some radical Jewish and Christian traditions. Each of these groups, generally, identifies with the term and uses it to describe and define different activities.

Women who are lesbians, feminists, Pagans, Jews, or Christians all may describe themselves as being "into women's spirituality," and to each it probably means a different thing. To the lesbian Witch and to a majority of Dianic Witches, it is likely to mean that she is participating in a religion which exalts and worships women's energy. To some feminist Witches and most neo-Pagans, women's spirituality may mean a tradition with a complementary blend of female and male polarities; while to Jews and Christians, it may mean identifying elements of their religion which they see as affirming to women. Even these broad definitions do not effectively address what may be meant by women's spirituality. Any one of the women mentioned may define or describe herself as participating in women's spirituality. Because of this, if you are unsure what a women means when she says "women's spirituality," it is better to ask questions rather than assume that you know.

There is some joy in knowing that many women are interested in what they consider women's spirituality, while at the same time this high level of interest can generate great confusion. It is to the credit of the women's spirituality movement that no one group has attempted to claim exclusively the term "women's spirituality," but it can also be a great frustration. Attending an activity, a class, or a ritual billed as a women's spiritual event may include any or all of the groups mentioned above. If you are considering attending an event, it is a good idea to clarify what women's spirituality means to that group before doing so. The same is true when discussing women's spirituality. It is wise to establish first if this term is being used in a common context.

▪ Feminist Spirituality

Some women who use the terms feminist spirituality or feminist Witchcraft use them in exactly the same context as women's spirituality, but to many of the women who define themselves as feminist Witches/spiritualists the terms have a more distinct meaning. Often women's spirituality connotes a more global grouping which includes both women who consider themselves feminists and some who do not. The primary difference between feminist spirituality and women's spirituality is that feminist spirituality includes a concept of the political and societal dimensions of religious practice. This is most often true whether a woman considers herself a Witch or not. Feminist spiritualists acknowledge a connection between the status of women in society and their status in the religions of that society. Religions which scapegoat, belittle, or oppress women and/or in which female deities are under-represented or non-existent are not considered feminist religions. Feminist spirituality is, then, a spirituality which is affirming to women and which acknowledges within the religion the basic tenets of feminist political ideology.

Feminist spiritualists often have one of two major reactions to traditional religious options: reject or reform. The feminist reformists, be they Christians, Moslems, Jews, or from other traditions, believe that the practices which oppress women are the result of secular patriarchy, and that a return to purer spiritual values by their tradition's practitioners will eliminate this oppression. In keeping with this analysis of the source of oppression, they work to reform the practices and current interpretations of their prophets. The second option, rejecting traditional religious choices, often leads women to explore the other major category of counter-culture spirituality, neo-Paganism, and to define themselves as Witches.

■ Paganism

"Paganism" is another broad term. It is used both by some of the women involved in women's spirituality and by others, female and male, involved in certain varieties of nature-based religions. These religions include, but are not limited to, the traditions of Witchcraft or Wicca. There are Craft traditions and individuals who consider themselves Pagans but do not consider themselves Witches. In spite of this, it is common for the terms Pagan and Witch to be used interchangeably by members of the Craft community. The term Craft refers to Witch "Craft" and is a common term used to distinguish Witches as distinct from Pagans.

The word Pagan is a reclaimed word. Like the word Witch, Pagan is a term which many find is invested with power. Even those who use the term Pagan as an insult often credit Pagans with having power, however unsavory. To reclaim a word is to claim the power associated with it and to restructure the values associated with the term into a positive framework. This process is similar to that of many lesbians who have reclaimed the word dyke. Dyke, formerly an insult describing a woman who appeared to non-lesbians as male-identified, is now commonly used by lesbian feminists to describe themselves. In the same way as the word dyke holds power for lesbians who define themselves as such, the word Pagan holds power for those who choose to identify with it.

Technically, any individual who is not a Christian, Moslem, or Jew is considered a Pagan. It is sometimes a shock to adherents of Native American traditions, Buddhists, Hindus and Bahá'is to find that they are counted in the ranks of Pagans. The neo-Pagan community, however, defines itself and is generally defined as individuals and groups who consider themselves a part of Witchcraft or other closely related traditions. The "neo-Pagan community" is another one of the vague classifications used to describe any number of persons and practices.

Neo-Pagan is used in this book to mean any of a number of practices and individuals who are part of the Pagan revival. In the late 1960's and early 1970's, there was a renewed interest in the religions which predated the traditional religious options of today and a re-emerging interest in the occult in both the United States and Europe. These two factors combined to produce a movement that has become known as neo-Paganism. Very few of the persons investigating these pre-existing religions were actually interested in adopting intact a religious practice from a pre-existing era. Instead they modeled a new religion on the old. These religious practices became collectively defined as neo-Paganism.

It is probably easiest to define the neo-Pagan community by identifying who neo-Pagans consider a part of it and who they do not. The individuals who define themselves as part of the neo-Pagan community do not actually consider Hindus, Buddhists, or Baha'is to be included within the definition. There is a willingness to and an interest in including Native traditions within the neo-Pagan community. There are members of the neo-Pagan community who consider themselves adherents of Native paths, but, at the same time, there are members of Native paths who do not choose to identify as neo-Pagans. Defining oneself as a neo-Pagan, as with most things in the neo-Pagan community, is considered to be a personal decision. Members of the neo-Pagan community use Pagan and neo-Pagan interchangeably. For the purposes of this book, both will be used to mean neo-Pagan.

Probably the largest portion of the neo-Pagan community consists of those who call themselves Witches, and, as already mentioned, "neo-Pagan" is often used interchangeably with the word "Witch." There are, however, neo-Pagans who do not identify as Witches. For example, the New Reformed Druids of North America* consider themselves neo-Pagans but not Witches. Among Druids and Witches there is often both a friendly banter about the different thealogical bases of their traditions and a comraderie of shared philosophy.

Paganism, like woman's spirituality, is a general term. Neo-Paganism, in generally accepted use, describes any of a number of non-traditional religions including, but not limited to Dianic,* Eclectic, Georgian,* Alexandrian,* Gardnerian,* Discordian, Feminist, Lesbian, and Native American* traditions. It also, like women's spirituality, may have any number of definitions, depending on who is using it and in what context it is being used. The best concrete information available about neo-Paganism is in Margot Adler's, *Drawing Down the Moon*, and if you are interested in learning more about the traditions and attitudes of neo-Pagans, it is an excellent and readable resource. Even Adler is often at a loss to categorize Pagans in any way, and states, "While these groups all differ in regard to tradition, scope, structure, organization, ritual, and names for their deities, they do regard one another as part of the same religious and philosophical movement."[1]

Within the neo-Pagan community there are probably hundreds of traditions. Although the distinctions are at times somewhat vague, each tradition, theoretically, represents a different philosophy, practice, and ritual style. These traditions fall, generally, into three categories: Traditional, Cultural, and Eclectic.

The Traditional groups include many different branches of what is considered "traditional British Wicca." Some of the most well known are the Gardnerian, Alexandrian,* Georgian* (each named for the man who "began" the tradition), and those of the New Wiccan Church including Silver Crescent, Modesto, and Kingstone. Unlike some other branches of the Craft, Traditional Wicca is most often considered to be a religion as opposed to a philosophy by its practitioners. In keeping with this distinction, being a part of a Traditional coven requires a strong commitment. One does not casually drop in to a traditional group. One becomes a formal member of the group and is, virtually always initiated into the coven.

The Traditional coven almost always follows a prescribed set of rituals with little variation and generally participates in these rituals skyclad (the Craft word for nude). Within these rituals, and in Traditional groups in general, there is a strong emphasis on the balance/polarity of the Goddess and God. Along with the other assets of Traditional groups, one of their real strengths is their emphasis on training those who are members of their covens. Most Traditional groups have a formalized training system with degrees to recognize rank and progress. These training programs often produce broadly educated, competent members of the Craft community.

Athough Traditional groups have many strengths and, in fact, much of the ritual practiced within neo-Paganism has been "borrowed" from them, they are also one of the strong sources of controversy within the Pagan community. This controversy has several causes. Probably one of the most profound is the alleged "secrets" of Traditional craft. Many of the rituals, beliefs, and activities within a Traditional group are considered priviledged. Members are not "allowed" to discuss them with those outside the tradition. They are expected to "keep the silence." This anomaly in the generally open atmosphere of the Pagan community is considered by many to be unnecessary.

Another area of controversy is caused by a perceived attitude on the part of some Traditionalists that their practice constitutes the "true" Craft and that the rest of Paganism is solely stolen bits of their ritual and practice. Although there may be some truth to the latter, the belief of some Traditionalists that theirs is the one true Craft can lead to an elitism which many others in the Craft find objectionable.

Finally, for feminist Witches interested in participating in Traditional Craft, there may be several barriers. Primary among them is that Traditional Pagans are far more likely to be traditional in other beliefs also. This includes acceptance of mainstream cultural attitudes about the "place" of women. Although a priestess is technically the "head" of each coven and, in fact, most Traditional covens trace their passing on of knowledge and power through a matriarchal lineage, some groups still remain male identified. Additionally, because many of the prescriptive rituals of Traditional Wicca place a strong emphasis on a male and female balance, same-sex magic is viewed as a minor heresy. This emphasis on female-male balance encourages a negative attitude toward same-sex couples and encourages heterosexism.

Another group of traditions that are commonly found in the Pagan community are those which are focused on the religions of different cultures. These traditions are based on whatever information is available about the religious and/or spiritual practices of a specific population. As one might imagine, these Cultural traditions can be very diverse. Some of the more common groups are based on Norse, Native Central American, Welsh, Native North American, Egyptian, Roman, Greek, and Africian beliefs.

Some Cultural traditions are considered Pagan but not neo-Pagan. These are traditions which attempt to adopt, as much as possible, the unaltered traditions of the indigenous people which they are choosing to use as a basis. The definition of neo-Paganism includes within it a presumption that a tradition may be based on an ancient or modern mythology but that it is being adapted by the group which is using it. Neo-Pagan Cultural traditions are those which use the myth and practices of another culture and form them into a spiritual practice that is styled for the life experience of the group. Cultural traditions seem particularly to attract people whose ancestors came from that culture. For example there is a large number of people of Welsh ancestry who are a part of Welsh Cultural traditions. However, there are also individuals who simply choose to identify with a tradition which has no relation to their ancestry. This, in many circles, is considered questionable. If, for instance, a group of white people choose to practice a cultural tradition that is from a black culture, they could be accused of co-optation. Choosing to follow a Cultural path that has nothing to do with one's personal heritage can be courting controversy.

The last and probably broadest types of tradition define themselves as Eclectic. These traditions pick and choose from any source that interests them to create their rituals and traditions. There are some real strengths to an Eclectic approach. It allows a group to select what they feel is the best of everything. Eclectic rituals are often diverse, and their practices are varied. At the same time, an Eclectic approach can be so broadly based that it has no focus and little meaning. Some Eclectic groups include a hodge-podge of different styles, cultures, and beliefs which do not produce a cohesive whole.

Despite these differences in traditions there are many similarities among Pagans. Most of the members of the "neo-Pagan community" hold some common values. Many are vegetarians, believing that matriarchal peoples were vegetarian. They may also follow a hierarchy in their choice of food. This hierarchy posits that fruits and nuts should be preferred foods because they are freely given with no pain involved. Next in the hierarchy are dairy products which, although they may be uncomfortable for the animal to provide, do not involve taking any life. The third choice is vegetables which are considered less extreme than taking animal life (even though their acquisition or consumption often involves killing the plant). Animals are last, and for many are not considered food at all. This does not mean that all Pagans are vegetarians. The Pagan ranks include many dietary choices including those who eat animals and those who would dispute the order of the chain just mentioned.

Another common value in the neo-Pagan community is a peace consciousness. Many neo-Pagans are pacifists and are also active in political peace actions. Among neo-Pagans there is often a political consciousness which closely parallels that of women who come to the Craft through feminism.

■ Women in the Craft and Mainstream Paganism

Within the neo-Pagan community at large, women are well represented. There are probably three women to every man in what is often called "mainstream" Paganism. Mainstream Paganism is a title that is given to any number of Pagan sects which are alternative in religious choice, but which are also somewhat more traditional in lifestyle than many feminist Witches. Mainstream Pagans defy almost all classifications. Some Pagans are poor, some are rich. Some Pagans are middle class; some are working class, some are upper class. Some have minimal education, while some have Ph.D.s. They are diverse in ethnic and racial background. Overall, there is no one type of Pagan, and about the only thing that they consistently agree on is that they disagree about almost everything.

For almost any statement that can be made about Pagans, one can find an exception. With this in mind, here are some general statements about neo-Pagans as they compare to the population at large.

Mainstream neo-Pagans are more likely. . .

–to live in extended family units, including friends and mutiple relationship partners;
–to have a tolerance for unusual behavior;
–to have once been hippies;
–to have a political consciousness;
–to be experimental;
–to read science fiction/fantasy;
–to own or have owned Volkswagens;
–to be non-monogamists;
–to be nudists;
–to have jobs which they value;
–to have an environmental consciousness;
–to be "low tech," but not "no tech;"
–to use or have used drugs, especially marijuana and halluci- nogens (both in and out of rituals);
–to be involved in some type of liberation philosophy;
–to have progressive attitudes about sex;
–to have different attitudes about their sexual, social, racial, and political ideology than the culture at large;
–to watch less television;
–to be avid readers.

When compared to those involved in women's spirituality, mainsteam Pagans are more likely. . .

–to be heterosexual;
–to live in nuclear family units;
–to follow traditional female and male roles;
–to have hierarchical religious structures;
–to wear costumes in their ritual;
–to have a belief in duality or polarity;
–to be more interested in the trappings/tools of Paganism;
–to be heterosexist;
–to have a consistent structure for their rituals;
–to initiate into the Craft;

–to have degrees or rank within the circle;
–to be "into the occult."

Most of the men in mainstream neo-Paganism are more progressive than their counterparts in traditional society. This, however, varies greatly from man to man, and one should not assume that because a man is neo-Pagan, he will hold progressed attitudes about women. There are Pagan men who actively work with the women in their lives to create equality in their relationships, and there are also Pagan men who are abusive to the women in their lives. As in the other areas of neo-Paganism, one should never make assumptions about the orientation or attitudes of its participants.

Women actively involved in women's spirituality, feminist spirituality, Dianic Craft, and/or lesbian Craft should not expect unconditional acceptance from the neo-Pagan community. When feminist Witches and, particularly, lesbian Witches began to identify with the term Pagan and to attend mainstream Pagan events, it caused great controversy. Mainstream Craft often includes a concept of ritual magic that "requires" female and male polarities. Some mainstream Pagans believe that it is not possible to have true magic with only women or only men. Women exposed to the Craft from within the women's community challenged this belief. Because most Pagans are progressive, the concepts of same-sex magic and of lesbians in a Pagan community were viewed as challenges which many faced with the courage and flexiblilty characteristic of mainstream Pagans at large. Some individual Pagans, however, still hold traditional cultural attitudes about women, lesbians, and gays, and continue to disapprove of same-sex ritual and magic.

Feminists and lesbians who have tried to take part in training in Mainstream Craft have often met with obstacles. Mainstream Craft training can include an orientation towards women, hierarchy, ritual, leadership, and sex that are not acceptable in most feminist Craft circles and certainly not to many Dianics or lesbians. This mainstream Craft view of magic demands that both women and men be included in all ritual and can occasionally include ritual heterosexual sex or the "great rite," as it is called in some traditions. If you are considering training in mainstream Craft, make sure that you learn all that you can about the training beforehand. Interview your potential teacher(s) and ask questions about their attitudes on the role of women and what the training will include. Ask direct questions about any sexual activ-

ity which may be involved, and don't ever be coerced into doing anything that you don't feel comfortable doing or that goes against your
instincts.

▪ *Woman-Centered Paganism*

Women's spirituality is not considered a part of mainstream Paganism,
and neither is most feminist spirituality, but there are woman-centered
traditions which are viewed by many as somewhat reluctant members
of the Pagan community. The classification of Wiccans as Dianics, lesbian Witches, and some practitioners of feminist spirituality brings
these women into what is technically the Pagan community. This
somewhat unlikely alliance is one which has a tendency to make some
women Wiccans and some Pagans (female and male) moderately
uncomfortable.

At the same time, women Witches went through the extensive process of refinement their philosophies from feminism, through unlearning, through the matriarchy to Wicca, only to find that some people
(and that includes some men) calling themselves Pagans had found the
Goddess before them. This was very disappointing for some. Regardless of this, both women Wiccans and mainstream Pagans have in the
past few years had continuing contacts. Feminist Witches have generated within neo-Paganism a new life and vitality, while mainstream Pagans have shared their traditional Craft knowledge, often absent from
many areas of feminist Witchcraft.

As mentioned before, not all members of the mainstream Pagan
community are comfortable with the ideas and concepts of women's
Wicca. Same-sex magic, lack of initiation rites, spontaneity of ritual,
lack of recognized leadership/hierarchy, and exaltation of the Goddess
are all interpretations/practices of Wiccan thought which stretch the
traditional meaning of Paganism.

▪ *Dianics*

This should not be construed to mean that there is total acceptance by
feminist Witches of the mainstream Pagan community. Most often only
a handful of women is willing to make the journey into the mainstream
Pagan community to gather knowledge and information, and some are
truly skeptical that anything gained from this source can be trusted.

Many women Witches who come from a feminist background define themselves as Dianics. Like everything else in women's spirituality and Paganism, the term "Dianic" is one which has several meanings. A majority of Dianics do not recognize male energy in their ritual, their magic, or their universe. These women feel they need psychic and spiritual space with only women's energy.

The rationale of the Dianics can be very compelling. If a goal of magic is to contribute to the world's balance, and if there has been an over-emphasis on male deities for at least the last two thousand years, then society and religion are out of balance. These women joyfully volunteer to do their part in restoring the balance by worshiping only female deities and working only with women's energy.

Dianics probably constitute the fastest growing group in the Pagan community. Thousands of women—young, old, feminist, lesbian, bisexual, heterosexual, and even mainstream Pagan—are beginning to identify as Dianics. They are coming to the Dianic tradition for every possible reason: validation for themselves as women, affirmation of their intuitive feelings, frustration with the men in their lives, frustration with traditional religion, direction for their psychic abilities, knowledge of the occult, out of a need for ritual in their lives, seeking others who share their perspective, and to find community. The Dianic tradition is alive with the possibilities of each of these women. It knows and follows no pre-defined structure or system. Most Dianics have no set process of initiation, few prescriptive behaviors, and no limit on creativity. It is a living and vital religion even in strict sociological terms.

There are actually three varieties of Wiccans who consider themselves to be Dianics. Probably the smallest group is mainstream Pagans who have a concept of both female and male deities and who (before it was common for feminist Witches to call themselves Dianics) identified with the ancient Celtic traditions which Margaret Murray identified in her books *The Witch Cult in Western Europe* and *The God of the Witches* as the Dianic tradition. Although I understand that this type of Dianic exists and even though Margot Adler documents their existence in *Drawing Down the Moon*, I have to say that in my many years in the Craft, I have never met anyone who identified as a non-feminist-based Dianic. I therefore cannot comment on them and their practices and beliefs.

The second common group of Dianics is similar to that of feminist Witches. They are of all sexual preferences, but primarily heterosexual or bisexual, women who have come to the Craft through feminism or through the women's movement. Although these women may be involved with men in one way or another, they still agree that religion has over-emphasized the male in the last several thousand years. They enjoy the company of other women and wish to share their spiritual energy in women's circles. These women may or may not participate in other activities in the Mainstream Pagan community, and may or may not participate in ritual or magic with men. The definition of these women as Dianic is one which seems to be evolving. The description of a non-lesbian woman as a Dianic is one which many "straight" women were reluctant to accept and which many lesbians rejected out-of-hand until only a few years ago. This is still a controversial issue within Dianic Craft.

The third group of Dianics is lesbian Dianics. Although these women may identify themselves as being "into" women's spirituality, as feminist Witches, as Pagans, and/or as Wiccans, Dianic is the primary term which lesbians use to describe "their" Craft. For obvious reasons, many lesbians are not interested in celebrating the existence of a male deity no matter how benign. Some of these women are very proud of participating in spiritual activities with only women and have a concept of "spiritual virginity."

Lesbian Dianics are the most active and visible of all those who call themselves Dianics. The lesbian press is full of dialogue and information about lesbian spirituality which, for many, is synonymous with Dianic Wicca. Z. Budapest's book, *The Feminist Book of Lights and Shadows*, published in 1976, defined feminist Wicca as Dianic. This book was widely circulated in the emerging women's community and, for many years, was the only information available about the feminist Dianic tradition. Although Z. did not identify the Craft as a lesbian religion, she did identify it as a separatist tradition, and this promoted the concept of Dianic Wicca as "the" religion of many lesbian separatists.

Lesbian separatists are women who choose to limit as much as possible their interactions with the male world, and often the women in it, in an effort to avoid the oppression which is often inherent for women in any such interaction. Separatism is not viewed as a negative action of excluding men but as a positive action of celebrating women. Lesbian Dianics, therefore, are seldom interested in working with mainstream Pagans due to the inclusion of men in their activities and their belief in male deities. Lesbian Dianics do, however, most often consider themselves Pagans. If traditional, conservative Pagans were right about the need for female/male polarity in magic, then magic would not work for lesbian separatists. This is simply not the case. Some of the most powerful and effective magic I have ever had the priviledge of being a part of has been conducted by women who consider themselves, in varying degrees, to be separatists.

The Dianics, grown out of the feminist movement, be they lesbians, lesbian separatists, or otherwise, constitute one of the most dynamic Pagan traditions today. It remains to be seen what balance will be struck between the Pagan community and woman-centered Pagan traditions. But with the integrity and openness of each of these groups, it will undoubtedly be an interesting and insightful process.

■ Eco-Spiritualists

Another group of people commonly found in the Pagan community is the Eco-Spiritualists. These are both women and men who have come to the Craft not through an identification with the occult, magic, or matriarchy, but because they feel an intimate connection to the Earth. This connection is so strong that they feel it as sacred and have sought connections between this feeling and their religion. Since Paganism is a religion which values highly the sacredness of the Earth, Eco-Spiritualists are naturally drawn to it. People who come to the Craft through a connection to the Earth are well represented in mainstream Paganism and are only slightly less well represented in women's spirituality. Paganism and environmentalism go hand in hand. It is difficult to be a Pagan and be unconcerned about nature (although this, like everything else in Paganism, is not always true). Sometimes Paganism breeds a belief in Eco-Spirituality, and sometimes Eco-Spirituality breeds Paganism. The two are highly complementary.

■ Women, Native American Traditions and Paganism

Practitioners of Native American traditions are represented in both the Pagan community and the women's spiritual community as well as outside the bounds of both. This is another vague term, and many neo-Pagans and women who consider themselves a part of Native American traditions cannot say exactly what it means. Some believe Native American traditions are the true spirituality of the Americas and that the importing of European and Eastern deities to these continents will never fit the energy patterns of the West. Further, there seems to be little conflict between the philosophy of most Native traditions and Wicca. In fact, the parallel nature of many Native American traditions and Wicca is cited as an example of a pre-historical, world-wide matriarchal religion which simply continued to be developed in different areas.

The case for this is quite convincing. The world views of most Native American spirituality and of Paganism are so similar as to seem to be extensions of the same thealogy. Wicca and many Native traditions have a parallel belief in the connectedness of all individuals and all systems in nature; they both have a concept of a Goddess; they each have a belief in the existence of energy to affect change—power to the Wiccan, medicine to the Native American; they have similar mythologies; and both include a belief in reincarnation. This belief is so strong that in many Native American cultures, there is no way to say good-bye—the assumption being that, of course, in one form or another, beings will meet again.

There are several groups which are based on Native American traditions which are considered to be on the periphery of Paganism. The Bear Tribe* in Washington publishes *Wildfire* and sponsors Medicine Wheel Gatherings, trainings, apprenticeships, and vision quests. Also, the Sunray Meditation Society* has a large following within some communities. Sunray is a combination of Cherokee traditions and Tibetan Buddhism combining chanting, visualization, and movement meditation. Sunray was specifically created as a vehicle to make available Native American teachings to non-natives.

Many books have appeared in the last few years which respond to the interest in Native American spirituality. Paula Gunn Allen's book *The Sacred Hoop* is an effort to reclaim the female roots of Native American traditions. In addition, Lynn Andrews' series (which includes *Medicine Woman, Flight of the Seventh Moon, Jaguar Woman, Crystal Woman,* and *Star Woman)* is written from the perspective of a white woman who is being educated about spirituality by Native women. For those who prefer reading fiction, Anne Cameron's *Daughters of Copper Woman* is insightful and inspiring while also entertaining.

For those women interested in becoming involved in Native traditions, some words of caution. Some Native traditions include what can be experienced as a subtle sexism. Some traditions contain little or no sexism. In addition, the judgement that some traditions are sexist is often based on misunderstanding or misinterpretation. There are, however, within many Native traditions definite ideas about the roles of women and men. Probably the best known example is barring menstruating women from participation in sweats. Feminist spiritualists interested in participating in the sweats immediately protested the inequity of being prohibited from participation in these ritual cleansing activities. However, from the Native American point of view, women are not prohibited because they are unclean during their cycle, but because they are already clean. Their bleeding itself is believed to fulfill the same function better than any sweat. Additionally, women are considered to be most powerful when they are bleeding, and contact or interaction with a bleeding woman renders men's magic/medicine ineffectual. Although a good case can be made for these traditions growing out of respect for women, at the same time it may prove difficult to justify these attitudes.

The use of the term "shaman" to describe non-Native practitioners of Native American traditions is also very controversial at the moment in the women's spiritual community. It is not uncommon to meet women who call themselves shamans. Some feminist Witches believe that shamanism is a term used to describe a particular brand of male magic and is not a good description of women's magic, Native American or otherwise. There are, however, women who feel that this is the best word to describe their practice because it includes the concepts of Witch, healer, visionary, and priestess all in one word. It remains to be seen whether this will be a word which will be reclaimed and accepted by members of the women's spiritual community or if its male association will prove too strong.

It is also true that not all Native Americans are interested in sharing their spiritual tradition. Settlers in the Americas have stolen, co-opted, and changed so much of the life and traditions of Native peoples that it seems only reasonable to refrain from intrusion into their spirituality. Native religions have, of course, already been contaminated by Western patriarchal ideology. The concept of the "Great Spirit," so popular in the old westerns, is, for many traditions, a new patriarchal concept imposed on matriarchal Native traditions. Do not expect all Native Americans to be interested in educating others about their spiritual traditions. If you are interested in learning more about Native American traditions, be prepared for conflict and controversy within both the women's spiritual community and the Native American community.

As one can probably detect from this chapter, most Pagans and those involved in women's spirituality are not terribly concerned with definitions. They are far more interested in participating in the rituals, discussions, and practices of the Craft than they are in knowing what people would call what they do. True definitions of what it means to be a Pagan or a member of the women's spiritual community may come later, but if the current trends continue, there will never be only one definition of these counter-cultural spiritual traditions.

■ *Resources*

Paula Gunn Allen, *The Sacred Hoop*. Boston: Beacon Press, 1986.
Lynn V. Andrews, *Medicine Woman*. New York: Harper and Row, 1983.
Lynn V. Andrews, *Flight of the Seventh Moon*. San Francisco: Harper and Row, 1985.
Lynn V. Andrews, *Jaguar Woman*. San Francisco: Harper and Row, 1985.
Lynn V. Andrews, *Star Woman*. New York: Warner Books, Inc, 1986.

■ *Traditions*

Alexandrians - see New Wiccan Church
Dianics - see Circle of Aradia; Re-formed Congregation of the Goddess; Susan B. Anthony Coven #1
Druid - see Ar nDraíocht Féin; Reformed Druids of North America
Gardnerian - see New Wiccan Church
Georgian - see The Georgian Church
Native American - see The Bear Tribe; Caney Indian Spiritual Circle; Sunray Meditation Society

■ *Groups*

Aquarian Tabernacle Church, Inc., Rev. Pete Pathfinder, P.O. Box 85507, Seattle, WA 98145. Group of Pagans who have chosen to serve and honor the Goddess and the God of the Old Religion through its own tradition of helping and stewardship; Retreat House and Center for Non-Traditional Religion; publishes *Panegyria* 8 times a year; mixed (female and male).
Ar nDraíocht Féin (ADF), Ad. Isaac Bonewits, P.O. Box 1022, Nyack, NY 10960. An Indo-European "reconstructionist" tradition of Neo-Pagan Druidism—emphasis on scholarly, artistic, ceremonial excellence. Nonsexist, nonracist, environmentally oriented; "Third Wave;" mixed.
Arachne, Ariana Lightningstorm, P.O. Box 5358, Laurel, MD 20707. Ever-changing group of women who get together about 4 times a year to share women's space, network, and do rituals; beliefs are varied; rituals worked out collectively.

Association of Cymmry Wicca, Lady Branwen, P.O. Box 1866, Athens, GA 30603. Followers of the ancient path of the Celtic Nations; correspondence course available for serious students; the Association is a group of covens and groves in US who worship as Pagans and Witches; mixed.

The Bear Tribe, P.O. Box 9167, Spokane, WA 99209. Sponsors Medicine Wheel gatherings, training, apprenticeship, and vision quests; publishes *Wildfire*; mixed.

Caer Rhiannon, Lady Angharad, P.O. Box 5261, Riverside, CA 92517. Network/clearinghouse for Pagans/Crafters in the Riverside-San Bernardino-Ontario area; training in the Outer Court tradition (other traditions among membership); mixed group; referrals to other area groups available.

Caney Indian Spiritual Circle, Spider, P.O. Box 6874, Pittsburgh, PA 15212, Tel. (412) 782–0987. Earth-honoring; celebrates full moon, solstices, and equinoxes with traditional Central American ceremonies; workshops; personal shamanic healing services; quarterly newsletter, *Moon Breath*; mixed.

Centre of The Divine Ishtar, P.O. Box 9494, San Jose, CA 95157, Tel. (415) 856–6911. Local (northern California-South SF Bay) Goddess worship fellowship with traditional eclectic/Wiccan focus; mixed genders; members of many traditions (Dianic, Gardnerian, Celtic, Eclectic, Qabalist, Santera, Culdee, etc.).

Church of All Worlds, Anodea Judith, 2140 Shatluck #2093, Berkeley, CA 94704. Neo-Pagan, Earth-centered organization which charters: Forever Forests (environmental activities); Lifeways (classes/workshops); Nemeton (publishing); Ecosophical Research Association (exploring the origins and actualizations of myths & legends); and Holy Order of Mother Earth (closed magic group); mixed.

Circle, P.O. Box 219, Mt. Horeb, WI 53572, Tel. (608) 924–2216. Legally recognized Wiccan Church with worldwide ministry that includes networking, festivals, healing, herb-crafting, counseling, workshops, residential training programs, legal marriage ceremonies, speaking tours, other services; publishes *Circle Network News*; mixed.

Circle of Aradia, Ruth Barrett, 41111 Lincoln Blvd. #211, Marina del Rey, CA 90292. A group of Feminist Activist women in the Dianic Tradition; open rituals several times a year for the women's community; sponsors occasional events & workshops.

Committees of Correspondence, Dee Berry, Coordinator of Clearinghouse, P.O. Box 30208, Kansas City, MO 64112, Tel. (816) 931–9366. Publishes *Greener Times* containing information about Green issues; key values include: environmental wisdom, grassroots democracy, personal and social responsibility, nonviolence, decentralization, community-based economics, postpatriarchal values, respect for diversity, global responsiblity, future focus; mixed.

Council of the Blue Moon, Railt, P.O. Box 27465, San Antonio, TX 78227. Eclectic tending toward Dianic; publishes *SheTotem*, a womyn's magic newsletter;

runs a lending library, and consider themselves service-minded to the Pagan community; womyn only.

Council of the Magickal Arts, Judy Carusone, 9707 Chatfield St., Houston, TX 77025, Tel. (713) 271–1154. Comprised of groups and individuals who meet at Beltane and Samhain to celebrate the God/ess in Light and Love; quarterly newsletter; mixed.

Covenant of the Goddess (COG), P.O. Box 1226, Berkeley, CA 94704. National confederation of Wiccan covens of various traditions (Gardnerian, Dianic, Celtic, Eclectic, Kingstone, NROOGD, Tanic, etc.); COG has Local Councils in various parts of the country; mixed.

Daughters of the New Moon, P.O. Box 65, Con.Sta. 6, 1525 Sherman St., Denver, CO 80203. Denver-area women meeting on the new moon, sharing knowledge and skills, bonding together, defining their femaleness through the religious impulse; not a coven, or Wiccan.

Elf Lore Family, Terry Whitefeather, P.O. Box 1082, Bloomington, IN 47202. An ecological folklore group; practices open-minded interaction among all species; holds festivals in Lothlorien, a land sanctuary; and publishes *Wild Magic Bulletin*; mixed.

Fellowship of Isis, Baron Strathloch, Hon: Olivia Robertson, Clonegal Castle, Enniscorthy, Eire. A multi-religious, multi-racial, multi-cultural fellowship dedicated to the Goddess of Many Forms; in 1987, FOI had 8,012 members in 59 countries; The College of Isis gives Magi Degrees through 16 Lyceums in 10 countries (including US); publishes *Isian News* quarterly; mixed.

Finnigan, Amy Baldwin, 3965 Seven Trees Blvd #204, San Jose, CA 95111, Tel. (408) 225–5108. A Celtic-oriented, eclectic, mixed group focusing on balancing Goddess and God energies in its members; "we honor the manifestations of the Goddesses and Gods within ourselves, joyously celebrate the seasons, work to develop our magical and psychic powers and commit ourselves to social action."

The Georgian Church, 1908 Verde St., Bakersfield, CA 93304. A church of Wicca in the Georgian tradition; publishes newsletter; mixed.

The Grove of the Unicorn, Lady Galadriel & Lord Athanor, P.O. Box 13384, Atlanta, GA 30324. American Eclectic Tradition; teaching/working/celebratory group focused on balance and personal evolution; ongoing classes available; sabbats open by invitation; mixed.

Mother Hearth, Spider, 222 Rad Nor Ave., Pittsburgh, PA 15221, Tel. (412) 782–0987. Eclectic women's spiritual path; combines elements of various traditions; celebrates the eight harvest holidays; meets for healing, divination work, and study; women-only; formerly Seedweavers Circle.

New Wiccan Church, National Office, P.O. Box 162046, Sacramento, CA 95816. Traditional British Wicca, Gardnerian, Alexandrian, etc.; Goddess and God worship; provides referrals to local groups throughout US; mixed.

Oakwind, Kyril, P.O. Box 64, Mt. Horeb, WI 53507. A Pagan grove for study, ritual and self development aimed at eventual initiation into a traditional coven; meets twice a month to study & worship together; mixed.

Of a Like Mind, P.O. Box 6021, Madison, WI 53716, Tel (608) 838–8629. An international organization of spiritual ♀ following positive paths to spiritual growth; provides services specially designed to network and aid communication among like-minded ♀; publishes *Of A Like Mind* newspaper quarterly; womyn only.

Oregon Pagan Association, c/o ASUO; EMU, Suite 4, University of Oregon, Eugene, OR 97403, Networking and ritual-oriented organization that enables Pagans and those interested in magick and the Goddess to contact each other; mixed.

Our Lady of Enchantment, Church of the Old Religion & School of Wicca, P.O. 1366, Nashua, NH 03061. Wiccan seminary; holds full and new moon rituals; celebrations on the quarter and cross-quarter days; training circles; Friday night public religious services; mixed.

Our Lady of the Sacred Flame, Judith E. Carusone, 9707 Chatfield St., Houston, TX 77025. A recognized church comprised of groups/individuals in the Craft; "primary mission to share our various traditions and to educate the community-at-large about who we are and what we do;" mixed.

Pagan Alcoholics Anonymous, Aidan or Julie, P.O. Box 9336, San Jose, CA 95157, Tel. (415) 521–6126. 12-step group for Pagans recovering, or attempting to recover, from alcohol and other substance problems; rituals and meetings also; mixed.

Pagan/Occult/Witchcraft Special Interest Group of Mensa (POWSIG), P.O. Box 9336, San Jose, CA 95157, Tel. (415) 856–6911. International network of persons interested in Wicca, ♀ spirit, Paganism, nature spirituality, esoteric lore, and related topics; publishes *Pagana* newsletter; non-Mensans welcome as associate members; mixed.

Pagans for Peace Network, Samuel Wagar, P.O. Box 6531 Station A, Toronto, Ontario, M5W 1X4 Canada. A loose network of politically involved Pagans and Witches active in peace, environmental, feminist, Native, and other movements; mixed.

Reclaiming, P.O. Box 14404, San Francisco, CA 94114. Feminist spirituality and counseling center; newsletter; magickal classes; mixed.

Re-formed Congregation of the Goddess, Inc., P.O. Box 6021, Madison, WI 53716, Tel. (608) 838–8629. A ♀'s religion dedicated to re-membering & re-forming the ancient congregations of the Goddess; publishes *The Crescent* newsletter; sponsors *Of a Like Mind* network and newspaper, The ♀'s Thealogical Institute, The Grove, conferences & workshops; womyn.

Reformed Druids of North America, Live Oak Grove, 616 Miner Rd, Orinda, CA 94563. Celtic traditions; new and full moon celebrations; Celtic High days; newsletter *Druid Missal-Any;* mixed.

Silver Acorn Circle, P.O. Box 850568, Yukon, OK 73085. Mixed, eclectic Wiccan group with many and varied interests (creative ritual, theosophy, philoso- phy, herstory/women's religions, smithcraft, etc.); scholarship and self- discipline emphasized; Sabbats open by invitation.

Silver Moon Circle, Lady Kayla, P.O. Box 2743, Redwood City, CA 94064, Tel. (415) 369–3154. Working circle; mixed group; various degrees; study/meditation Thurs. nights; full moon circles; teaching, metaphysical and Craft; open for study and/or membership.

Sisterspirit, Women Sharing Spirituality, Frodo Okulam, P.O. Box 9246, Port- land, OR 97207. Women of all traditions come together in celebration of our commonality as spiritual women; rituals, workshops, and kindred groups (Wiccan, Christian, Jewish, New Age, etc.).

South Bay Craft Teachers, P.O. Box 9336, San Jose, CA 95157, Tel. (415) 856–6911. Network of Wiccan teachers in the San Jose/Peninsula/Santa Cruz area; many traditions (Mohsian, Fairy, Dianic, Gardnerian, Celtic, Eclectic, etc.); single gender and mixed groups; classes and Moon circles held separately according to the respective traditions; teachers and their groups join to share Sabbats.

Sunray Meditation Society, P.O. Box 308, Bristol, VT 05443. A combination of Cherokee and Tibetan Buddhism which includes chanting, visualization, and movement meditation; mixed.

Susan B. Anthony Coven #1, P.O. Box 11363, Oakland, CA 94611, Tel. (415) 653– 4169. Dianic; publishes *Thesmophoria* newsletter; Z. Budapest, High Priestess; women only.

Women in Constant Creative Action (W.I.C.C.A.), P.O. 5080, Eugene, OR 97405. Provides the means by which women can meet together locally in small groups, for supportive spiritual growth and metaphysical learning.

Women's Spirituality Forum, Z. Budapest, P.O. Box 11363, Oakland, CA 94611, Tel. (415) 444–7724. Produces Goddess lecture series, Halloween Spiral Dance, Annual Goddess Conference, and retreats; newest project: a God- dess Cable TV show! Performers, writers, producers, etc. welcome.

■ Notes

1. Margot Adler, *Drawing Down the Moon*. Boston: Beacon Press, 1986, p. 3.

CHAPTER 4

Making
Contact

For most women, being a Witch is a quiet avocation. Spiritual feelings are often difficult to talk about even with others who are known to share a common framework. Attempting to find others with whom one can share spiritual and/or occult thoughts may prove particularly difficult for women new to the Craft, or for those relocating to a new area. It is not generally something that you put up signs about in the local grocery or ask the woman next to you in the laundromat. Identifying where Witches are in your area and connecting with them can be a difficult and at times disheartening task.

Our culture has socialized us to respond with hesitancy to people who are "into the occult" or spiritual pursuits, and this at times can be valid. I'll never forget the first woman I met who said that she was a feminist Witch. She showed me her broom and her tarot cards, acting dramatically and suspiciously all the while. Her behavior was exactly what I had been socialized to expect from "Witches." Her view of the Craft was not the least comforting, and she seemed overly interested in impressing me with veiled references about her access to what seemed like manipulative power sources. "If this is feminist Witchcraft," I thought to myself, "this is not what I had in mind when looking for my spiritual path."

I learned later that, as in many other areas of the feminist community, there is a wide diversity about how the Craft is perceived and practiced in women's circles. Some circles are serious, sincere, and political, while others are playful, joyous, and celebratory, and some contain all of these qualities. If one is trying to find others with whom to share spiritual activities and thoughts, be prepared for diversity. Never assume that if you know one Witch, you know them all. The range of women practicing the Craft and the way they practice it vary so widely that it is difficult to designate any specific groupings. The Craft is a religion which prizes individuality and, as might be expected, has attracted and promoted individuality among its members.

There seem to be three basic types of feminist Craft practices. They are the ritual practice, the cognitive practice, and the integrated practice. This is not meant to imply that there is a definite division in feminist Craft, only that as women's spirituality has emerged since the mid-seventies, it seems to have three major forms or practices. Most feminist groups attempt to be integrated with a blend of ritual and cognitive practices. Any one group can contain Witches of both orientations, but a majority seem to emphasize one form of practice or another. A general description of what to expect from each type follows.

■ *Ritualists*

Ritualism is probably the most prevalent practice within the women's spiritual community. Ritualists celebrate the seasonal holidays, new moon, full moon, beginning menstruation, ending menstruation, trysts, handfastings, bondings, births, deaths, healing, or almost any special event with a ritual appropriate to the occasion.

Participating in rituals can be very moving. It can serve as a connecting link to the cycles of the earth and to women's lives. When well done, rituals awaken deep feelings and revitalize an awareness of the unique spark of divinity which lies in each of us. Rituals link together body, mind, and spirit. The elements of ritual are designed to stimulate all the senses: incense for smell, wine or juice for taste, special clothes and varied motions for touch, chants for sound, and a vast set of different symbols for visual impact. They engage the entire body in the actions of linking with the life force energy, both internal and external.

If ritual appeals to you, then you might consider joining a ritual group. There are three common varieties of ritual practice: the public ritual, the open group, and the closed group.

Public Ritual

Neo-Pagan organizations, feminist groups, and even some of the more progressive Christian churches sponsor public ritual. Neo-Pagans and feminists offer exclusively Pagan celebrations, while Christian groups often offer a "reclaimed" liturgy which, although still Christian-based, has been modeled after Pagan ceremony. Public rituals are large community events in which the number of participants can range from a dozen to a several hundred. Public rituals may be held on every holy day or may be organized for a specific event or function. Any person may attend, whether they identify as a Witch or not. Feminist groups often include only women, but ecumenical Christian groups and neo-Pagan organizations may include both men and women in their rituals.

The experience of a large group ritual can be dramatic. Several hundred people focusing on world peace or nuclear disarmament can carry with them a wave of energy that is almost tangible. Participation in public ritual generally carries with it few requirements. The group comes together for a specific event or purpose and has no expectation for further participation. Depending on the group, the focus of the ritual, and the participants in it, public rituals can range from dynamic experiences to seeming free-for-alls. It is often best to find out what is planned before you attend a public ritual, but in general, public ritual is one way to check on what is happening in your community, who is doing it, and what ritual can be like.

Open Groups

Open groups are another variety of ritual practice found within the women's community. These open groups may be sponsored by an existing group or organization and/or may be offered by an individual who is knowledgeable about the Craft. These groups may be called introductory classes, spiritual support groups, a grove, spirituality groups, therapy groups, or may be groups for a specific sexual orientation (e.g., lesbian spirituality group). The options which are available to you will vary from area to area, but, in general, you should determine if you are interested in participating in a group with women and men, a women-only group, or a group which shares your sexual preference, and seek out that type of group.

The expectations for open groups vary. Some may be time-limited, and your continued participation is expected for that specific period of time. Others may be open, and you can attend whenever you choose. If you are new to the Craft, new to your area, or are looking for new friends who share a common spiritual interest, open groups are one of the best ways to get to know other spiritual women in your community. If you are looking for a group to join, and you are in touch with the women's community at all, probably the best way to find such a group is to ask your friends. If your friends don't know, watch the feminist, Pagan and/or lesbian press, check the classified ads in more traditional newspapers, listen for public service announcements on the radio (especially if there is an identified women's station or show), and watch community bulletin boards.

If you are still not able to find any contacts in your area, you might want to try one of the Pagan networks. There are several networks which specialize in helping Witches find each other. *Of a Like Mind**

(OALM) is an international network for spiritual ♀. It has an extensive networking system with a computerized data base which includes ♀ who are community contacts for their areas. *OALM* offers a networking hotline for quick referral. It also publishes a quarterly newspaper and a sourcebook of contacts within the ♀'s spiritual community. *Circle Network News** publishes a neo-Pagan quarterly newspaper and a guide to resources in the Pagan community. The Circle Network is targeted to a mixed audience (women and men) and carries information primarily about mainstream Craft with an occasional feminist article and/or contact.

If you can't find any indication of activity in your community around women's spirituality, you may want to consider starting a group. Tell your friends and use the same outreach methods mentioned above (announcements in the feminist, Pagan and/or lesbian press, classifieds, public service announcements on the radio, and/or community bulletin boards) to identify other women who share your interests. Many women who have tried this have been surprised at the positive response. You don't have to know all about the Craft to start a group. You can find others and figure it out together.

Closed Groups

Closed groups often grow out of open groups. Frequently, members of an open group who have agreed to meet for a specific amount of time will want to continue meeting. Sharing ritual and spiritual contact seems to encourage bonding among women, and when the initial commitment to an open group is over, many of these women may want to continue working with and getting to know each other. The level of intimacy and the intensity among the participants in an open group can be dynamic, and continuing to work and celebrate together emerges as a priority for the members.

A closed group is often called a coven and generally has no more than twenty members. Many closed groups or covens serve multiple functions for their members. The women in them may consider themselves family, a support group, a social group, and/or peer counselors for each other. Members of covens and closed groups develop a special chemistry. A careful balance is built which includes trust, respect, and validation for each of the group members as individuals. Because of this, covens and closed groups are often reluctant to admit new members. If you are interested in joining an already organized coven or closed group, it is important to respect the previous interaction and work of the women involved. It may be that they will feel that the balance will be upset by the introduction of another member. If this is true, then see if they will allow you and/or a couple of friends "guest passes" for a few weeks or months. If that is not possible perhaps that group or some members from that group would be willing to help you in starting a group of your own.

■ Rituals

Most public and open rituals are primarily celebratory and spontaneous. The planning (if any) provides only a minimal structure to the celebration. Open and public group rituals generally involve chanting, dancing, and other activities designed to raise the energy level of the participants. The sounds created in these ritual groups are often forceful and vary from yells and screams to moans or quiet hums. Energy directed at these events most frequently has a general purpose on which a majority of the participants can agree, for example, energy for healing the earth, stopping nuclear proliferation, or easing world hunger. These larger group ritual activities can be quite intense and the energy generated can be dynamic. They can kindle, excite, and arouse the participants with their animated activity.

Different from the public or open group ritual, the activities of the coven or closed group are more personal. The participants are well known to each other, and the rituals are individualized and intimate. Although these groups are also often spontaneous, closed groups many times seem to develop a pattern for their rituals. Meeting on a regular basis provides a context, through knowing both the women one is working with and the type of activities common for the group. The interaction and energy of a closed group are as intense as that of the open or public group but in a different way. Covens or closed groups often deeply touch the participants, encouraging bonding and community.

The use of a priestess varies widely from group to group. Some more traditional circles, particularly those where some members of the group have been trained in a more mainstream Craft tradition, will have a designated high priestess who is in charge of preparation for and carrying out the ritual. In many circles the responsibility and priviledge of priestessing is shared or rotated among members of the group in some manner. If the meeting place rotates, the hostess may also be the priestess of that ritual, or it may be as simple as proceeding in alphabetical order through the women in the group. In other circles there may be no designated priestess at all. In this case, either all the ritual participants or some specific set of women conduct certain parts of the ritual. Each of these systems has advantages and disadvantages. If you are considering joining a ritual group, it is wise to attempt to find one that practices a leadership style with which you are comfortable.

While rituals can be dynamic and powerful experiences, rituals which are not well constructed or not well thought out can be anything from boring to frightening. Rituals read entirely from books, done without feeling, or done in a prescribed way are, most often, uninspiring and can even be dull. Although women's circles have been and continue to attempt to be inclusive, there are often barriers to some individual women's participation. Many circles make assumptions that all women are going to be comfortable with touching, hugging, and/or even kissing strangers. These activities may prove particularly difficult for women who are recovering from any type of assault. Many times, able-ist assumptions may be made, that all women can move around, dance, tell direction, or sit on the floor with ease. Assumptions that all women can tolerate incense or other strong smells are also common. If you have any concerns about participating in a ritual, it is best to discuss them beforehand. Ritual proceedings are generally not kept secret from the participants (with the exception of some initiation rites), and you should feel comfortable with and understand what is going to happen before you agree to participate. Women with mobility and/or personal issues should be sure to discuss them with the group before you find yourself in the middle of a ritual in which you cannot participate. If there is a designated leader/priestess, you can share your concerns with her rather than with the entire group if that seems easier. It is true that this can be difficult and that it does put the responsibility of communication on the woman with the challenge, but most circles are responsive to women's special needs and will attempt to structure activities so that all can participate. Those who are organizing rituals can also facilitate group sensitivity to individual needs by being open to questions during the explanation of what will occur, or, better yet, by asking directly whether any women present have any issues about touching, movement, allergies, etc.

In the past, most circles were not open to observers. Although you may still find circles which hold to this custom, this attitude is changing. Many circles now reflect the approach of some Native American traditions in which ritual is a part of the life of the Tribe. Observation, supportive non-participation, attending to children, and entering and leaving the circle as need and comfort dictates are becoming more accepted. The traditional prohibition about not breaking a circle, once cast, are being challenged as women bring ritual into their lives and mold it into an experience affirming to them.

If you are new to a circle or new to the Craft, make sure that you are comfortable with the women you are going to practice with and with their type of magic. If you find that you can't be involved in a ritual unless you are willing to be a full participant, ask for information about the orientation of the group (positive is all I'd recommend), the sexual orientation of the members (if that is important to you), and the form and activities of the ritual itself. Participating in a ritual in which you are not comfortable, do not comprehend the symbolism or don't understand can range from a frightening to a frustrating experience. Most circles will respect your concerns.

Often serious ritualists are women who are kinesthetic. Many of these women experience connections to their spiritual resources most deeply when their whole being is participating. The act of moving their bodies through a ritual is what awakens their spiritual energy. They connect with cosmic energy through ritual and draw from ritual direction for their daily lives. Magic is ritual and ritual is magic to most ritualists. Within the women's community today, these women are creating powerful, beautiful rituals alive with the symbols of women and the Earth. There are, however, some limitations to a kinesthetic-based practice of the Craft. Although ritualists may create moving experiences for the body, they cannot always articulate why it works, what will happen, where the symbols came from, what they mean, or how they were chosen. Ritual creation to them is often an intuitive process, rather than a rational one. Some ritualists are not easily verbal, and framing the words which are needed to communicate about ritual work proves a tedious and uninteresting process. They rely on the women from the second variety of feminist Craft practice to interpret and articulate what is going on. These women are cognitive practitoners.

■ Cognitive Practitioners

Although some ritualists are cognitive practitioners and some cognitive practitioners are ritualists, most women (and the groups that they are comfortable in) seem to have a leaning one way or the other. Cognitive practitioners are women who connect with their spiritual energy primarily through an intellectual process. If the intellect can conceptualize the practice of Wicca, the body and the spirit can follow, bringing with them a dynamic connection to internal resources.

Wiccan Thealogy and the Cognitive Practitioner

The work of the cognitive practitioner is strongly based on the thealogy and philosophy of women's Wicca. Although much of this information was shared in Chapter 2, a brief review of some of these concepts might be helpful. Feminist Wicca implies a series of values. These values include: the sacredness and connectedness of the Earth to all her plants and creatures; a high value on self-governance; a structure that places the needs of an individual over the needs of a society; and a belief in a continuing cycle of birth, life, and death, which includes a concept of reincarnation.

There is only one law or rule in Wicca, and it is called "The Rede." Traditionally stated, The Rede is, "And ye harm none, do as thou wilt." Cognitive practitioners attempt to become proficient in the *practice* of magic, or the bending of reality to conform with will, within the parameters of The Rede. The Rede expresses a code for how one may live her life and provides a basis for how situations may be handled. The practice of magic encourages a process of self-definition that is integral to Wiccan thealogy, and The Rede gently poses the moral question of what constitutes harm.

Most Craft traditions reflect strongly the principle of self-governance by an individual. The Craft has no specific book to study, no great woman (or great man) who is thought to embody the principles of the tradition. It is therefore not possible to emulate or mirror the actions of another individual, great or otherwise. Wicca is a self-defined religion, which puts responsibility on the individual to identify for herself what is right and wrong in any situation. Because Wicca is a religion which prizes individuality, it is paramount that any definition of Wiccan beliefs or tradition is not dogmatic. With attention to these principles, we proceed to the practice of the cognitive practitioners.

The task that cognitive practitioners undertake is difficult. Cognitive practitioners wish to explore the nuances of the cultural, political, and mystical dimensions of women's religion. Foremost among these difficulties is defining a spiritual practice without creating dogma. Although the Craft is an individually defined religion, many of the women practicing the Craft want definition. Those new to the Craft often want to know the "rules," without realizing that any rules that apply are internal and not external. Women working with cognitive groups attempt to awaken and/or identify their own internal morality and values. They discuss and share how other women's magic has worked and what outcome was generated by a certain action. This is not meant to encourage others to make similar decisions or take similar actions, but to share insights about how a situation might be handled. As one may surmise from this, any attempt to define the "one and only true women's religion" is blocked by the nature of the religious philosophy itself.

The Practice

The cognitive practitioners see Wicca as a life path. Witchcraft or "The Craft" becomes truly what is implied in the name: the art and practice of Wicca as a skill or craft. The situations, attitudes, actions, and decisions of daily life become a practice ground for the honing of these skills. Wicca, the ancient Craft of the Wise, provides, even within its simplicity, guidelines and parameters for the development of a personal, political, and spiritual framework. The ethical development of their Craft is the major thrust of the cognitive practitioners.

Cognitive practitioners often enjoy exploring the nuances of philosophy and thealogy. They attempt to define for themselves a working cosmology, placing personal and linguistic values on the concepts of women's religion. The cognitive practitioners are most often verbally fluent. Words, concepts, and ideas constitute the foundation of their cosmos. Discussion and interaction with others who can assist them to build a framework for their Craft is a primary factor in the development of their Craft practice. The interaction and discussion among cognitive practioners can be quick and energetic or deep and insightful, depending on the topic. Words form the basis of their magic. Most cognitive practioners seek Words of Power. The effectiveness of their magic depends on their ability to clearly articulate their goals, hopes, desires and aspirations. They engage in dialogue with others "of a like mind" to refine their concepts and attitudes as a basis for how they will choose to direct their energy. The more clearly they can state the exact essence of what it is they wish to become reality, the more clearly it manifests.

The Cognitive Group

The cognitive practitioners try to articulate the spiritual thoughts, feelings, and thealogy of women's Witchcraft. They are involved in research about the matriarchy, women's religion, Amazons, comparative religions, women's role in society, cosmology, ethics, Goddesses, divination, ecology, politics, auras, crystals, psychic skills, magic, and many other subjects. In general, at most "meetings" of cognitive groups there is a topic or a focus. This may be a book that is under discussion by the group or an identified topic. If you are interested in attending, you can generally find out ahead of time what will be discussed.

Cognitive groups are most often open discussions, study groups, book review groups, work groups or support groups. There are many similarities between cognitive groups and ritual groups. Cognitive groups can be open or closed, depending on the needs of the women involved and the structure of the group. Some consider themselves covens, while others may define themselves as a study or support group. The bonding and connection among the members can be similar to that of a ritual group. Also, as with ritual groups, the expectations among members may vary from one of family, to support group, to social group, to peer counselors. Although many of these groups also depend on the special balance built among the members, they are often more open than ritual groups to attendance by non-members unless the topic being discussed is personal or otherwise sensitive.

Also similar to ritual groups, the leadership pattern within cognitive groups varies. Some include an identified scholar who may emerge as the discussion leader, while others rotate leadership among topics or issues using the expertise and skills of the individual members. Some groups determine collectively what topics will be covered, while others have a curriculum which is established by the group organizer before the group begins. Becoming a part of a cognitive group is similar to getting into a ritual group. The same techniques are used to search one out. If you are interested in joining a cognitive group review the suggestions about finding and joining a ritual group given previously in this chapter.

■ *The Integrated Practice*

There are, within the women's spiritual community, groups which incorporate both ritual and cognitive practice. In the past truly integrated groups were somewhat rare, but they are now becoming more common. As cognitive practitioners have defined what it means to be a feminist Witch and ritualists have refined women's ritual practices, some groups have adopted a successful blend. This wealth of information about the practice of women's religion was not available in the early years of feminist spirituality. With new access to knowledge about what it means to be a feminist Witch and an understanding of ritual, the opportunity to adopt an integrated practice has become more of a possibility.

These integrated practitioners realize, as do most of the ritualists and the cognitive practitioners, that any attempt to value ritual activity over the intellectual conceptualization of Wicca or vice-versa would go counter to Craft teachings. Each of these groups has value. The ritualists have things to teach the cognitive practitioners and the cognitive practitioners can often explain the activities of the ritualists. In the future, the integrated group may become a more common third choice for women exploring their spiritual options.

■ *The "Witchie-in-the-Night Syndrome"*

Before continuing, it may be wise to offer some words of caution about what is not a fourth practice, but an occurrence that is common enough to be worth noting. As in any other spiritual or philosophical discipline, there are women in feminist Wicca who are a bit misguided or self-impressed and who define themselves as feminist Witches. They are most often unclear about their motives for being involved in the Craft. Generally, their reasons for interest may be well-intentioned but are misdirected. It may be because their friends or lovers are doing it, because they feel it will give them power, or because they have an exaggerated sense of the dramatic. The woman mentioned previously as the first Witch I met unfortunately had what I have learned later to identify as the "witchie-in-the-night syndrome."

If you are new to the Craft and are attempting to make connections, it will probably be useful to be able to identify the "witchie-in-the-night sydrome." It should be made clear that there is only a small need to be suspicious and that a majority of the women practicing the Craft are sincere. If, however, you should suspect that you have encountered a woman or group with "witchie-in-the-night syndrome" (WITNS), here are a few tips that may help you identify them.

1. WITNS types are seldom well educated about the Craft even though they may have been participating in activities related to the Craft for some time.
2. WITNS types often don't speak for themselves when asked a question about the Craft. Their answers are: "My friend, lover or *the* charismatic leader of our group says. . . ."
3. WITNS persons don't take responsibility for themselves. They often are looking for or have found within the Craft a "guru" who will give them answers and direct their lives for them.
4. WITNS types engage in exaggerated occult activities. At best this can involve a harmless form of extremely dramatic portrayal of events, and at worst it may include manipulative activities of some sort. If you suspect that a person has WITNS, be cautious of information or assistance that may be offered to you. Healings, psychic information, seances, tarot readings, or any number of other "secret" activities may be cited as the source of information all of which have the following outcome: The person being manipulated is informed that there is *one answer*, and it is *the answer* that is being given by the WITNS person. The WITNS person may also threaten that if you do not follow the advice, "dire circumstances" will befall you.
5. WITNS types in truth feel that they have little personal power and believe that their association with the Craft will give them unlimited power.
6. WITNS persons may dress strangely. It should be noted that many of what would be considered "normal" Pagans dress outside the current social norm in larger society. For a Pagan to have "power clothes," be they ritual items or unusual street clothes, is not uncommon. The WITNS person, however, may wear these

clothes inappropriately to impress others, not to put herself into a ritual frame of mind. Additionally, the clothes are often accompanied by exaggerated, dramatic behavior.

7. The WITNS type may use karma as a ploy. The WITNS person may try to convince people, especially those for whom the WITNS person feels a sexual attraction, that they have shared some past life karma with her. This karma must be addressed or more "dire circumstances" will befall the other individual.

Generally, these are the common behaviors of the WITNS person, although not all WITNS types exhibit all of the attributes mentioned above, and some of them will exibit none. If you suspect that you are dealing with a WITNS person, there are several ways you may want to proceed. If you feel that the WITNS person is misguided or is simply behaving this way because she lacks exposure to more appropriate Craft models, helping her to identify other options may be appropriate. If you are knowledgeable about the Craft, you may want to share information with the WITNS person in hopes that she will want to modify her behavior. If you are new to the Craft, then perhaps you can both look for others who can assist to educate both of you about the Craft. If, however, it seems that the WITNS person is making a conscious decision to behave in a WITNS way and is reluctant or refuses to consider other forms of behavior, then it may be wise to limit your interaction with her. If you at any time find that you are dealing with someone who identifies as a negative practitioner or Satanist, then the advice given in Chapter 3 still applies—leave.

■ Religious Organizations and "Churches"

The question of structure is one which brings interesting responses within the Pagan community. Some Pagans believe that the success of traditional Paganism rests on its anarchical small group/coven approach and that any attempt to organize and structure Pagan groups may jeopardize this success. Those who favor organization have different attitudes from those of the more traditional Pagans in several ways. First, the advocates of organizing feel that Pagans have been denied the rights of organized religion. Formally acknowledged marriages/bondings, funerals, Wiccanings (dedication of a baby to Wicca), legal ministers, and tax-exempt status are a few of the priviledges of organized religion which, thus far, are not often enjoyed in Pagan circles. Second, the organizers dispute that all structures are, by nature, rigid and believe that Pagans can create structures and systems that validate Pagan beliefs while encouraging personal freedom. Those who favor organization have begun to create systems that they hope will show that structure in and of itself need not be repressive.

Because of definitions within the Internal Revenue Service Code which govern application for tax-exempt status, organizations are forced to define themselves as either churches or religious organizations. These are not definitions which easily fit many Pagan traditions, and the title "church" is one which many Pagan organizations identify with reluctantly. When using this title it is important to be clear that to be a Pagan "church" is in most cases very different from being a traditional "church."

There are, at this writing, several groups that are attempting to provide some structure to alternative spirituality. The Covenant of the Goddess (COG)* is a coalition of individual covens which include both women and men, as does Ar nDraíocht Féin,* while The Re-formed Congregation of the Goddess* and Women in Constant Creative Action* currently focus on women.

COG was incorporated in California in 1975 as a non-profit religious organization and is an excellent example of an alternative structure which promotes individual freedom and yet provides a system of contact and communication among many diverse Pagan groups. Membership in the Covenant of the Goddess is "open to established Goddess-worshipping Craft covens [and individuals] of all traditions . . . ."[1] Its major goal is "to increase cooperation among Witches, and to secure for Witches and covens the legal protection enjoyed by members of other religions."[2] COG considers itself a national confederation of covens and solitaries, each of which subscribes to COG's ethical code. Several feminist groups, including the Susan B. Anthony Coven #1, of which Z. Budapest is High Priestess, are a part of COG. The COG confederation provides a loosely woven structure which allows great autonomy on the part of its members, while encouraging ethical practice and interaction among Craft practitioners.

The Re-formed Congregation of the Goddess Inc., (RCG), unlike COG, does not see itself as a religious organization, but as an actual spiritual congregation. The Congregation is an international women's religion providing the benefits and recognition of organized religion to its members. Its purpose is to foster positive spiritual growth among all persons, particularly women. RCG provides a spiritual, ethical, and social structure essential to validating women's experience.

The Congregation is incorporated in the State of Wisconsin and recognized as a tax-exempt religion by the Internal Revenue Service. Like COG, membership in RCG is governed by an ethical code called the Affirmation of Women's Spirituality (see Chapter 2 for information on the Affirmation). In addition, members must define themself as being on a positive path to spiritual growth. Membership in the Congregation is possible on an individual or a group basis. RCG considers itself an international religion which provides communication and spiritual development services for isolated members as well as groups and local members.

Despite its title, Women in Constant Creative Action (WICCA) does not actively define itself as a Wiccan group. Its focus is strongly on women's spirituality, which includes but is not limited to Pagan traditions. WICCA "provides the means in which women can meet together locally, in small groups, for supportive spiritual growth and metaphysical learning. These small groups are called WINGS. Each month the members receive from WICCA suggestions for their weekly meetings, and the potential ways in which these suggestions may be used. Members also receive a Study Packet, to use at their own energy, and may attend all retreats and gatherings. Classes are also held and are open to members."[3] Their name, they say, gives some indication of how they plan their future and was chosen to honor the fore-mothers of WICCA. WICCA is based in Oregon and a majority of its activities take place in the Northwest.

Another group providing an organizing function in the Pagan community is Ar nDraíocht Féin (ADF). At this time, Ar nDraíocht Féin is not tax-exempt but has plans to become so in the near future. Ar nDraíocht Féin, which means Our Own Druidism, is a tradition of neo-Pagan Druidism. It encourages excellence among its members, which include women and men. It is a tradition which is linked with "scholarship in the fields of linguistics, Indo-European studies, comparative religion, archaeology, anthropology, Celtic & Norse & Baltic & Slavic studies, history, musicology and polytheology."[4] Currently, it has several groves, with its main operations coordinated by Isaac Bonewits in New York.

These groups represent what may be a trend in Paganism. Many organizations and even individual covens are expressing interest in legal incorporation and tax-exemption. I believe this echoes the desire of many Witches today who believe that the time for women's religion and Paganism to be recognized religious options has come.

■ Conferences and Gatherings

Many of the groups mentioned above and some others sponsor conferences and gatherings for women and/or Pagans. If you are interested in meeting other Pagans, learning about different traditions, attending workshops, or meeting people who have been active in the Craft for years, conferences and festivals provide an intense exposure to Pagan culture and thought.

Women's Conferences and Festivals

The oldest conference which has a spirituality component is the National Women's Music Festival,* now held on the University of Indiana campus in Bloomington, Indiana. The National Festival was started in 1974. It is held on the grounds of the university, and the 1,000–1,500 women who attend generally stay in dorm rooms, other campus facilities or camping grounds. The primary activities of the festival are workshops and women's music. Since the early eighties, the workshops have been organized in several "tracks" or interest areas. These tracks include writing, the women's music industry, women's spirituality, and a general track. National was the first, and remains the only, multiple-function women's festival to have a specific track dedicated to women's spirituality. The purpose of the track system is to allow participants to mix and match interests and topics or to concentrate entirely on one interest area. Participants can choose to attend only workshops dealing with women's spirituality, or they can attend workshops on other topics of interest to them. The National Festival generally brings in several well-known women's spirituality writers/practitioners as speakers. This festival, although open to the general public, is attended almost exclusively by women.

Probably the most well attended and the most well known of all women's festivals is the Michigan Womyn's Music Festival.* The Michigan Festival has been held every August since 1975 in western Michigan. One major difference between the National Festival and the Michigan Festival is the accommodations. The Michigan Festival is held on 640 acres of unimproved land. Every year, several months before the Festival, women begin arriving and build all of the facilities (such as showers, stages) for the 5,000–8,000 women who attend. All women who attend (with the exception of some of those who are differently abled) camp in primitive settings for the five days of the Festival.

This festival is focused on producing and performing womyn's music, but like the National Festival, it is a multi-purpose festival with an extensive craft area, workshops, support facilities for women with disabilities or who are recovering from addictive behaviors, jam tent, and multiple concerts. The Michigan Festival is a strongly lesbian-identified festival, and a majority of the women who attend are lesbians. No men are permitted to attend. Unlike the National Festival, there is no specific emphasis on women's spirituality at the Michigan Festival. There is, however, a strong presence of spiritual women, and many of the workshops presented are of a spiritual nature. The day before the actual start of the festival there are intensive workshops lasting all or half a day. Many of these are on spiritual topics. The Michigan Festival (like National) also brings well known feminist spiritual authors and practitioners to conduct these workshops.

During the actual weekend of the festival, other workshops occur in both the mornings and the afternoons, and quite a few of them include spiritual topics of many types. Any woman may organize and present a workshop at the Michigan Festival, so the level of knowledge and the sophistication of the presenters, as well as the topics covered, vary widely. Michigan is an intense experience for almost every woman who attends, and many of the participants find it to be a spiritually significant event in their lives.

The Festivals mentioned thus far all have a similar purpose and style. However, the "Womyn and Witchcraft: Dianic Wicca Conference,"* sponsored by the Re-formed Congregation of the Goddess, is organized to fulfill a very different function. This event is held in Wisconsin and attended by 80–100 women. The facility in which the Conference is held is a residential group camp with bunkhouse style cabins. It is strongly lesbian-identified like the Michigan Festival, but is attended by a mix of women of different sexual preferences.

The purpose of this Conference is to generate discussion on philosophical and thealogical topics. There is little comprehensive information that explores the thoughts of women who consider themselves to be Dianic, and this Conference is designed to stimulate and gather information about the practice of Dianic Craft. It is not a "how to" conference. There are topical discussions related to the issues of women's spirituality from a Dianic perspective. The women who lead these discussions are identified Dianics, some of whom, like those at other festivals, are published authors, however, others are women whose primary qualifications are that they are active Dianics.

Still another type of conference is held each year at the University of Minnesota in Mankato.* This conference, like the National Festival, is held on the grounds of a university, but unlike the National Festival, it is devoted entirely to women's spirituality. The Mankato Conference is truly an ecumenical affair. It is attended by women of many different spiritual paths including Bahá'i, Zen, Native American, Jewish, Christian, (both Catholic and Protestant), Wiccan, and other denominations. The Conference is held over a weekend, and the activities vary from day to day. On Friday evening there are generally non-structured activities, and workshops begin on Saturday. The workshops reflect the diversity of the women attending, and the vast majority of them do include a spiritual focus. A well-known feminist author is often the opening speaker on Saturday. Saturday evening may include a concert and Sunday morning is dedicated to ritual activities. The ritual choices may include a "New Age" Christian ritual, a traditional Christian ritual, and a Wiccan celebration. This conference is most amazing in its ability to bring together women of diverse spiritual paths and successfully integrate them into the activities of the conference.

Pagan Festivals

Different from the women's festivals, Pagan festivals include both women and men and are attended primarily by those who consider themselves Pagans. These festivals have a different focus and feeling from women's festivals. Before attending a Pagan festival, it may be wise to consider some information about Pagan men. Although many call themselves feminists (and are in general educated about feminism) the assumption that all Pagan men will be accepting of a totally Goddess-oriented Craft, or of women as equals, is false. Men in attendance at Pagan festivals vary, as do the traditions they come from. They range from the very conservative to the very liberal.

The Covenant of the Goddess* sponsors the COG Grand Council and Merry Meet Festival every September. The site of this Festival moves each year to a different area of the country. Recent sites have been in New England, in the Midwest and on the West Coast. It is generally attended by about 450–500 people. For these people, the primary accommodation is camping. Many of the activities at the COG Festival have to do with the activites of COG itself. The Festival is a connecting link among the many diverse groups which make up COG. The Grand Council of COG actually meets during the Festival. This meeting includes the general business of the organization, such as reports from committees, reports from the different regions, policy determinations, and election of officers. In addition to the activities of the Grand Council, the Festival also has what is called Merry Meet, filled with rituals of every kind: rituals for the sunrise, rituals for the season, rituals for women only, rituals for men only, rituals for planetary healing, and many other types and varieties of celebration. Add to that workshops, song fests (bardic circles), crafts, and general merrymaking, and the true nature of the COG Festival and Grand Council begins to emerge.

The International Pagan Spirit Gathering* is sponsored by Circle Sanctuary and has been held in southern Wisconsin for years. A majority of the persons attending are Midwestern Pagans, but there is a scattering of Pagans from around the country. Pagan Spirit is attended by around 300 people of many Pagan traditions. It is held on a site which requires primitive camping. The structure and activities of Pagan Spirit are similar to that of the COG Merry Meet Festival. There are many rituals of a similar nature, daily workshops, singing, crafts, and any number of other casual activities.

Unlike the feminist festivals, there are no recognized speakers at these Pagan festivals. Both the COG Festival and Pagan Spirit include well known authors, organizers, and performers in the Pagan community, all of whom attend of their own volition, rather than being "the main speaker." At Pagan Spirit every year, the program lists "resource people" attending the gathering, but there are not designated "stars."

If you are considering attending the COG Grand Council, the Pagan Spirit Gathering, or the Michigan Womyn's Music Festival, you should be comfortable with nudity. Although it is by no means a requirement, many of the festival participants go "sky clad." If you are considering attending one of the gatherings open to women and men, be prepared to encounter nude persons of both sexes. In general, the nudity at these events is considered of little significance. Easy conversations and interactions are held between people in varying stages of dress and undress.

This is by no means a total listing of all of the festivals (either women's or Pagan) which occur. It is, however, a listing of those that are well known or have some distinctive notoriety. Other women's festivals include the New England Women's Music Retreat, the Southern Women's Music and Comedy Festival, the West Coast Women's Music and Comedy Festival, Womongathering, and the Midwest Women's

Festival. Smaller Pagan festivals are too numerous to mention. If you are interested in attending a festival or conference, watch the Pagan, women's, and/or lesbian press for announcements.

■ *Spiritual Correspondence Groups*

If you are not ready for or cannot attend a Conference or gathering, perhaps a Pagan pen pal may provide the contact and continuity you want and assist you in your Craft development. There is currently an option available for women interested in corresponding with other women. Nan Hawthorne's *Circles of Exchange* provides a round robin correspondence exchange for its members based on topical interests or geographic location. If you are interested in joining a round robin whose primary interest is, for example, tarot, *Circles of Exchange* can assist you to communicate with others who share that interest. If you want to correspond with women in other areas of your country or around the world, *Circles of Exchange* may be able to connect you with them too.

No matter what your level of interest, there are options available to you within the women's and Pagan communities that will enable you to connect with others who share your spiritual beliefs. Witches are coming out of their broom closets and redefining the tradition of silence about Craft activities. If you wish for others to share in your spiritual journey, you may find them right in your community or you may find them around the world.

■ *Resources*

Networks

Of a Like Mind (OALM), P.O. Box 6021, Madison, WI 53716, Tel. (608) 838–8629. An international network for spiritual ♀ with an extensive networking system, a computerized bank of ♀ who are community contacts for their areas, a networking hotline for quick referral, a quarterly newspaper, and a sourcebook of contacts within the ♀'s spiritual community.

Circle Network News, P.O. Box 219 Mount Horeb, WI 53572. Neo-Pagan quarterly newspaper and a guide to resources in the Pagan community.

Organizations

Ar nDraíocht Féin, P.O. Box 1022, Nyack, NY 10960.
Circle Sanctuary, P.O. Box 219, Mt. Horeb, WI 53572.

Covenant of the Goddess, P.O. Box 1226, Berkeley, CA 94704.
Re-formed Congregation of the Goddess, P.O. Box 6021, Madison, WI 53716.
Women in Constant Creative Action, P.O. Box 5080, Eugene, OR 97405.

Conferences and Festivals

Canadian Women's Music Festival, 161 Stafford St., #2D, Winnipeg, Manitoba, Canada R3M 2W9.
Covenant of the Goddess Grand Council and Festival, P.O. Box 1226, Berkeley, CA 94704.
Elf Lore Family Festivals, ELF, P.O. Box 1082, Bloomington, IN 47402.
Mankato Women's Spirituality Conference, MSU Box 64, Mankato State University, Mankato, MN 56001.
Michigan Womyn's Music Festival, WWTMC, P.O. Box 22, Walhalla, MI 49458.
National Women's Music Festival, P.O. Box 1427, Indianapolis, IN 46207.
New England Womyn's Music Retreat, P.O. Box 217, New Haven, CT 06513.
Pagan Spirit Gathering, P.O. Box 219, Mt. Horeb, WI 53572.
The Southern Women's Music and Comedy Festival, 807 Onslow St., Durham, NC 27705.
The West Coast Women's Music and Comedy Festival, 15842 Chase St., Sepulveda, CA 91343.
Womongathering, RR5, Box 185, Franklinville, NJ 08322.
Womyn and Witchcraft: Dianic Wicca Conference, P.O. Box 6021, Madison, WI 53716.

Correspondence Exchanges

Circles of Exchange, Nan Hawthorne, 4807 50th Ave. S., Seattle, WA 98118. Round robin letter exchange.

■ Notes

1. Covenant of the Goddess, brochure.
2. Covenant of the Goddess, brochure.
3. *On Wings*, Vol. 5, Number IV, back cover.
4. Isaac Bonewits, "What Ar nDraíocht Féin Will and Won't Be," *The Druids' Progress*, Report Number 1, p. 5.

CHAPTER 5

Divination

■ What Is Divination?

From the beginning of time, women have sought ways to gain information about their environment, their lives, their loves, their livelihoods, and their relationship to the Goddess. In cultures which were/are closely connected to their matriarchal origins, divination nearly always plays a part in the spiritual activities of the community. Native American spiritual practices include divination by aeromancy, alectryomancy, and alomancy (see list below). The Greeks were particularly fond of prophecy, while the Celts and Central American natives practiced scrying. Judging by the materials available today, prophecy seems to have been the most common of ancient divinatory forms. Most of the ancient prophecy practices appear to have included a type of ritual which was thought literally to draw down the Goddess into a woman who then spoke and answered questions on behalf of the deity. Although prophecy is not the divinatory style of choice in the women's spiritual community, women of spirit are rapidly reclaiming divination as a major tool of the Craft.

The range of divination and divinatory tools is both wide and deep. Just a few of the options open to one who would consider divination are:

1. Acuto-manzia–divination with pins.
2. Aeromancy–divination from the air and cloud shapes, comets, etc.
3. Alectryomancy–divination by the actions of birds.

4. Alomancy–divination by the throwing of salt and reading the patterns that it creates.

5. Apantomancy–divination based on the meeting of animals, (e.g., black cat crossing one's path).

6. Cartomancy–divination with cards/tarot.

7. Cartopedy/Solistry–predicting the future and assessing character by the soles of the feet.

8. Scrying/Crystal Gazing–divination with crystal ball, dark mirror, or water.

9. Dowsing–the art of finding information by means of a stick, metal rod, or pendulum.

10. Hydromancy–divination by observing water's color, ebb, or flow.

11. Numerology–divination with numbers.

12. Palmistry–divination by the lines in a person's palm.

13. Pendulling–divination by the movement of an weighted object (a pendulum).

14. Physiognomy–divination by assessing the shape of the face.

15. Runes–divination with stones, chips, etc., inscribed with magical symbols.

16. Graphology–the study of handwriting.

The list doesn't stop here, but includes many more forms of divination like Ouija boards, tea leaves, I-Ching, and even bone-throwing.

Divination has been and can be used to attempt to generate all sorts of information from the grand to the most mundane. The type of information received and its accuracy often surprises those new to the divinatory arts, and it can continue to amaze even those who have used divinatory systems for years. There is healthy skepticism in the women's spiritual community about divination: where the information comes from, how much of the information is filtered through the values of the reader (i.e., the person doing the divining), and questions about the wisdom of acting on divinatory information. Although some women of spirit do not technically "believe" in divination, there seems to be a general acceptance of the idea. Most seekers seem to feel that where the information gained through divination comes from is not important if the information has relevance in one's life and can be used to assist in making decisions and taking action.

■ *Divination and Cosmic Theory*

If, (as discussed in Chapter 2), life is not a series of random accidents but, instead, a series of synchronistic occurrences, then information about these patterns should be accessible with certain tools or prescribed actions. In addition, if all time is now, then on some level the information which one is seeking is available in the present. Divination seeks to break down the barriers of time and space and to use the intuition and psychic abilities of the querent (the person with the question) and/or the reader. The proponents of the divinatory arts believe that there is a "cosmic information source," be that internal or external to the querent, to the reader, or to the divinatory process. They tap into this information by using something which heightens or masks the senses and which allows this information to be communicated to the querent.

Divination is frequently considered/attempted by women who are seeking direction. Our culture often removes us from many of the more natural ways to gain information about our role in the cosmic dance, while presenting extremely complex situations and providing little context or time for resolution of these situations. The Vision Quest, sweats, fasting, chanting, and meditation—all traditional ways of reconnecting with this cosmic energy force—are still not in common practice in the women's community (although they are re-emerging).

Most divinatory arts are accessible to women regardless of their knowledge of the Craft, income, or level of education. With a little study and/or practice, divination can become an accessible tool which fits within the constraints of our fast-paced world.

■ *The Hazards of Divination*

There are two common hazards in divination. Like almost anything else, it can be abused. It can be abused personally, and it can be abused by someone seeking to manipulate the querent. People with compulsive personalities or individuals who are personally insecure can become divination junkies. These women cannot act without advice from their cards, coins, or pendulum. This behavior can include two or three I-Ching consultations a day, using a pendulum for making even small decisions, keeping a tarot deck by the phone for quick information about whether or not to answer it, and many more compulsive behaviors. In most cases, the divination junkie is harmless to everyone but herself. However, there are some times when one might be personally concerned. These include: when what you supposedly did in a past life begins to be the basis of present action by the divination junkie or other community members; if the divination junkie practices divination which includes other people and behaves frantically unless information gained through divination is acted upon or insists that her advice be followed; or if she becomes disenchanted with divination because it gave her the "wrong answers" and misplaces that anger on the other women whom she perceives have duped her into "believing" in the system. When these types of behavior occur, then the divination junkie is no longer harmless and should be approached with caution.

The second hazard of divination is the poor or manipulative reader. It is important to ask questions and be comfortable with anyone whom you choose to assist you in seeking information through divination. Many readers/counselors have strongly held personal agendas or philosophies. These can range anywhere from interpreting information within a strong, traditional religious context to attempting to manipulate the querent to engage in certain behaviors or actions which will be of benefit to the reader. For women seeking to reclaim their own spirituality, caution should be taken with any reader who is attempting to direct your actions without giving you the right to interpret the information and to make decisions on your own. Particularly common in these categories are admonishments about lesbianism, the Craft, political action and non-traditional lifestyles. Be wary of any reader who breeds fear or encourages dependence.

Divinaton is a powerful tool which can be used for either positive or negative ends. Use your intuition. What you feel about a person or system is probably valid. Be sure that you are comfortable with any divinatory system that you choose to use and with whomever you might choose to practice.

■ Psychic Skills and Divination in the Women's Community

It is almost impossible to speak about divination without dealing with the view of psychic ability within the women's community. As mentioned in the previous section, most members of the feminist spiritual community are hesitant to be strongly identified with the traditional occult. Seances, table tapping, contact with the dead, and other forms of traditional occult practices are all uses of psychic energy which are viewed as suspect and which are not commonly used. Even less dramatic uses of psychic ability, such as mediumship, channelling, crystal gazing, or contacting one's spirit guides are often used with hesitation. It has been and remains important within the feminist community for all forms of spirituality to be accessible and practical, for the practices of womanspirit not to be alienating to other women, and, even more strongly, for these practices not to be or appear to be foolish.

At the same time, women's intuition and the concept that every woman is psychic is taken very seriously. Many women are drawn to the Craft in search of tools for using and controlling their psychic selves. These women are seeking positive ways to develop and use their psychic talents. Most types of divination provide an excellent framework for the development and use of innate psychic abilities, and women of spirit have used divination to recognize and validate the non-rational information that is gained from psychic insights. Accepting and learning to use information gained from an intuitive, right-brain perspective is an important part of many Craft teachings. As mentioned in Chapter 2, the ability to perceive and understand intuitive information is considered one of the best bases for taking action. Since divination is most often attempted when seeking information about a possible course of action, the knowledge gained from a psychic source forms an integral portion of any divinatory consultation. Divination is one of the tools which validates our intuition and which allows us to communicate with the less-commonly-perceived realms.

Before we go any farther, it would probably be wise to define the word psychic. If one were to ask any group of ten women what they believe it means to be psychic, one would probably receive ten very different answers. Being psychic for one woman can mean the ability to send and/or receive non-articulated information from another person; for another it may be the ability to know events before they happen; and for yet another it may be the ability to gain information about a person from their personal belongings. There are probably about as many definitions of psychic abilities and behaviors as there are women who have considered defining psychic skills. A partial list of psychic skills:

1. Psychic Artist–a person with the ability to psychically perceive and channel images and transfer them to paper or other media.
2. Animal Reader–a person with the ability to understand and interpret the psychic signals of animals.
3. Auric Reader–a person with the ability to see and interpret auras.
4. Automatic Writer/Automatist–a person with the ability to communicate psychic information in writing—often, but not always, used in connection with non-form beings.

5. Boosters/Amplifiers–persons with the ability to increase another person's psychic powers/signal.

6. Blockers–persons with the ability to limit psychic activity/transmission.

7. Broadcasting Empath–a person with the ability to send and/or inspire feelings in others.

8. Clairvoyant/Seer/Second Sight/Vision/The Sight–a person with the ability to see or the act of seeing non-form or non-present energy.

9. Clairaudient–a person who hears non-form or non-present energy.

10. Psychic Composer–a person with the ability to perceive and channel musical information.

11. Dowsers–persons with the ability to use kinetic energy to generate specific information (i.e., location of water, lost items, answers to questions, etc.).

12. Psychic Dreamer–a person who has meaningful dreams and/or the ability to interpret dreams.

13. Empath–a person with the ability to pick up the feelings/emotions of other people.

14. Finders–persons with the ability to locate lost persons or articles.

15. Fiscal Reader–a person with the ability to predict the movement of the stock market/investments, etc.

16. Fixers–persons with the ability to fix machines, computers, equipment, etc. with information not available from a rational base.

17. Healers–persons with the ability to assist others to initiate their own healing processes.

18. Intuition–the apprehension of an idea by the mind without the intervention of reason.

19. Latent Psychic–a person who has psychic ability but who suppresses it or is unaware of it.

20. Levitator/Psychokinetic/Telekinetic–a person with the ability to move objects or direct energy with only the power of the mind.

21. Mediumship/Channelling–the ability to speak with or for non-form beings.

22. Pyros–persons with the ability to know where and when a fire will break out and, at times, to exert control over a fire.

23. Patterners–persons with the ability to see and/or create patterns, generally on a large, objective scale.

24. Plant Reader–a person with the ability to understand and interpret the psychic signals of plants.

25. Psychometry–the ability to pick up vibrations and information from objects.

26. Precognition/Premonition–a knowledge of future events based on intuitive feelings.

27. Prediction–the ability to foretell events, trends, etc.

28. Prophecy–the ability to receive divine revelation.

29. Receiver/Sensitive–a person with the ability to perceive the thoughts/feelings of another person.

30. Sender/Broadcaster–a person with the ability to send thoughts/feelings to another person.

31. Psychic Surgeon–a person with the ability to perform medical procedures, often without medical training or instruments.

32. Telepath–a person who has the ability to send a psychic signal perceivable by a majority of people regardless of their own psychic abilities.

33. Teleportation–the ability to produce or move objects without any mechanical means.

34. Units–a group of persons whose psychic signal is increased by using their psychic skills in coordination with other specific people.

35. Psychic Vampires–persons with the ability to tap or draw on another's psychic energy without their consent.

36. Xenoglossia–the knowledge of a language one has never learned.

Based on this list, it is hard for me to say if divination is based on psychic skills or if psychic skills are a part of divination. A case can be made for either. Whichever is the answer, women have chosen many kinds of divination as the training ground for psychic development and validation of their own intuitive knowledge. The emergence of divination has been primary in the development of feminist spirituality, rivaled only by the development of ritual. In a society which has taught us to deny our reality, it is not surprising that women of spirit have found ways to validate themselves, their actions, and their intuitions through divination.

A Brief Explanation of Three Types of Divination

Divination as practiced by women of spirit seems to fall into three basic groups. These are: 1) divinatory systems based on a random generation of information from kinetic contact with a preset system of symbols; 2) divination using psychic skills; and 3) divination using a scientific base, (some might not identify these as divination at all).

Divination has been a major focus of the women's spiritual community since its beginning. Women have devoted a lot of energy to the development of divinatory skills. Much of the information offered either by the women's spiritual media or at conferences about women's Wicca will be "how to" information about a specific divinatory system (most often one with a psychokinetic base). Since the late seventies, women have generated a tremendous amount of knowledge about divination and have created their own body of literature and tools for using various divinatory systems. Women of spirit have developed their favorite systems which are affirming and accessible to seekers whether these women are just beginning or are well along in their spiritual journeys.

■ Psychokinetic-Based Divination

A majority of the most popular divinatory systems currently in use within the women's spiritual community have a psychokinetic base. Among these systems are Tarot, I-Ching, Dowsing, and Runes. The assumption when using psychokinetic divination is that unconscious kinetic energy communicates information through a divinatory tool. These divinatory systems contain a preset series of symbols for which, in most cases, a preset definition has been established. Divinatory systems with a kinetic base have little chance of interference by the conscious mind in the process of divination and call for little personal responsibility on the part of the reader or the querent. The women's spiritual community has been hesitant to leap directly into the realm of the traditional occult, but psychokinetic-based divinatory systems which do not rely on overt psychic abilities and which can be practiced by most women are quite popular.

Tarot

Probably the most popular of all divinatory systems within the women's spiritual community is the tarot. The tarot is a very accessible divinatory tool. It is available in gift shops, in women's, New Age, and occult stores, in traditional and women's decks or with specific ethnic and/or regional symbolism.

What can one expect when consulting the tarot? Using the tarot is quite simple. The querent (the one seeking information) formulates a question, and shuffles the cards. The reader then lays out the cards in a specific pattern which reveals information about the question asked.

The tarot is an excellent tool for awakening insight. A traditional tarot reading does not give specific answers to the question. It instead relates attitudes and feelings about an issue which helps the querent herself to identify intuitive information of which she was perhaps not aware. Yes and no answers in a tarot reading are not generally possible unless you are using a system like the one described in *Choice Centered Tarot* by Gail Fairfield or in *Motherpeace* by Vicki Noble. Some of the very things that make the tarot so appealing are the same things which can, at times, make it frustrating. The tarot does not often give specific or explicit direction. It is often said, "When considering what type of divination to use: if you want insight use the tarot, if you want direction use the I-Ching." The tarot can and most often does generate an amazingly accurate description of one's feelings about an issue, but for those who are fairly clear about their feelings to begin with, the tarot may seem redundant.

The language of the tarot. The tarot speaks to seekers in a symbolic language. It uses visual cues to assist in the awakening of the deep mind of the querent and/or the reader. There are two primary tarot systems being used by women: one which could be called gestalt tarot, and second, a system which includes a specific, preset definition for the symbols of the cards. Both of these systems have merit and, at times, are even used alternatively by the same reader. Examples of a preset system of symbols can be seen in the Rider-Waite deck and in other decks in which the symbolism is very consistent. For example, whenever mountains appear on a card, they indicate knowledge, water is symbolic of intuition, and cups deal with issues of love and fulfillment. These preset definitions for the symbols allow the reader to respond to the querent's question by applying her knowledge of this pattern of symbolism to the cards in a reading.

"Gestalt" tarot is not based on a preset definition of the cards but is based on the querent's reaction to the symbols of the cards. This use of the tarot relies strongly on the psychic/intuitive skills of the querent. It holds that the symbols in the cards will intuitively register with the individual consulting the tarot, providing them with the information that they are seeking. It also holds that the symbols in the tarot are archetypal and that they elicit a similar response from many women without any information about traditional meanings. This form of consultation uses both the kinetic energy of the querent in shuffling and choosing the cards and the intuition available to the querent about the cards in relation to her question. The querent is guided by the reader to answer questions about the cards using the acknowledged or unacknowledged psychic ability of the querent. As women are and have been seeking acknowledgment of both their feelings and their psychic abilities, the symbolic language of the tarot validates and encourages knowledge of the self and intuition.

The women's spiritual movement and tarot. From the beginning of women's spiritual explorations the tarot has been the most used divinatory system within the women's spiritual community. This was a tool that could be reclaimed by women and used with relative ease. During the early period of the feminist spiritual movement, women spent a considerable amount of time creating feminist tarot interpretations. Knowledge of feminist tarot was primarily an oral tradition with information passed from individual woman to individual woman. These women sought to take an existing patriarchal tarot system, remove the parts which continued to promote patriarchal thought, and then read tarot which was affirming to women's experience.

Anyone who has attemped to read or learn from mainstream tarot interpretations will know how they encourage a traditional world view. This view often includes only heterosexual definitions, traditional relationship patterns, patriarchal religious choices, and other values which differ greatly from those in the feminist community. Out of frustration with these traditional interpretations, women began to develop their own interpretations of the cards. Included within Z. Budapest's book, *The Holy Book of Women's Mysteries*, was a basic description of the use of the tarot and definitions for the cards from a feminist perspective. This was closely followed by Sally Gearhart's interpretations in her book *A Feminist Tarot.** At that time, as there were no women's tarot decks, Gearheart's book used the traditional Rider-Waite deck and reclaimed the cards with interpretations which were meaningful within the feminist community. Both of these books made significant contributions to the development of feminist tarot.

Billie Potts, River Lightwomoon, and Susun Weed created the first actual women's deck, *The Amazon Deck*. In 1978, Billie Potts also published *A New Women's Tarot.** This book was and remains one of the most affirming tarot interpretations for lesbian feminists. *The Amazon Deck* (which is no longer available) was brilliant in many ways but was also difficult for some women to use. The cards are alive with symbols relevant to women and to women's experience; however, because they were created by many different individuals, there is no consistent symbolism.

This deck was only a beginning. Dozens of feminist decks have since come into being. Ffiona Morgan's *Daughters of the Moon Tarot* and *Shekhinah's Tarot* by Shekhinah Mountainwater are only two of the many women's decks now available. In 1983, Vicki Noble and Karen Vogel created the *Motherpeace Tarot*. This deck and the accompanying book, *Motherpeace: A Way to the Goddess through Myth, Art and Tarot,** are probably the most popular tarot system in use in the women's spiritual community today. *Motherpeace* is a round deck and, as such, seems more consistent with women's cyclic perceptions. The symbolism and interpretations are truly affirming of women's experience and can serve as a powerful tool to link women to the matriarchal origins of the tarot.

Another book which provides copious information about the matriarchal origins of the tarot is Barbara Walker's book, *The Secrets of the Tarot: Origins, History, and Symbolism.** Although these decks and interpretations are not strictly women-only, they provide dramatic concepts of the matriarchal basis of tarot.

The Winged Chariot* is a tarot newspaper which is directed toward feminist interpretations of the tarot; within the larger spiritual movement, the *Tarot Network News** is a semi-annual newsletter with information about the tarot. The *Of a Like Mind* newspaper occasionally has a tarot column and provides networking information to women interested in sharing the tarot, and *Goddess Rising* also has articles on tarot.

The tarot is a powerful divinatory tool which can be used by the beginner and by the adept of womanspirit. The reclaiming of tarot has been refined by women of spirit and one can now find feminist decks and interpretations with relative ease. A woman seeking an accessible and reliable system of divination can trust the new feminist tarot systems to enlighten her and awaken her intuitive self.

The Reclaiming of the I-Ching

General information about the I-Ching. The I-Ching is another psychokinetic-based divination system now popular in the women's spiritual movement. It is considered an oracle (which means it is a source of knowledge or opinion). The name of the oracle, "The I-Ching," literally translates from the Chinese to mean "The Book of Changes," and it is thought to be one of the oldest existing written documents. Many feminist spiritualists believe that the origins of the I-Ching predate its writing (credited to Fu Hsi in third millennium, B.C.E.) and that the written I-Ching does not reflect the matriarchal, Goddess orientation of oral I-Ching.

The advice and opinions offered in the I-Ching are based on what can be easily identified as matriarchal principles. The I-Ching details the relationship of the elements as they interact with each other. It reflects the observation of the planets and the responding effects of the tides. It shows a sensitivity to the nature of animals and an understanding of the lifeforce of plants. Underlying it all is a strong consciousness of the cycles of nature and the oneness of all life.

Despite these basic matriarchal values, the traditional I-Ching does not value or validate women's experience. The development of the traditional I-Ching spans many centuries and includes the philosophies of many different male Chinese authors. It grew to include not only values of the relationship of the cycles and the elements of nature but also the concerns of the Chinese patriarchy.

A traditional I-Ching includes advice on the lesser place of women in the society and in the family. It encourages humility and an acceptance of one's destiny, even if that destiny is to be poor and oppressed. It promotes the values of society over those of the individual and reflects the traditional Chinese social structure with the father as patriarch and the eldest son as his successor. The youngest daughter is symbolic of a person with no power, and the marrying maiden who assertively pursues her own partner is suspect. It details relationships and styles of hierarchal government, and advises the wise use of warfare.

Obviously, this paradox led many women of spirit to look to the I-Ching for information and advice and, at the same time, to be repelled by the blatant patriarchal ideology upon which parts of it were seemingly based. Many women chose not to use the I-Ching at all because of this. Others chose to reinterpret it, changing the "superior man" to the "progressed individual," or the "youngest daughter" to the "newest feminist." As a result of this attraction/aversion, the I-Ching has only begun to be reclaimed and reinterpreted by feminist Witches in the past few years.

What can one expect when consulting the I-Ching?   Unlike the tarot, the I-Ching is usually very direct. It speaks in much more specific terms. It can advise one to stand still, to make no response, or to be assertive; it may also inform you that the situation is really over and that no further energy should be spent on it.

Also unlike the tarot, the I-Ching is more often a solitary pursuit. Although many women read tarot for themselves, there is also a great tradition of "having your cards read." The I-Ching, however, is most often consulted by a woman on her own. She may choose to ask for assistance in interpretation from friends, but, largely, the responsibility for interpretation rests on the individual consulting the oracle. Using the I-Ching does call on intuition. The words on the page have little use unless the reader has insight into how they address her question.

The I-Ching is based on a series of straight and broken lines. These are used to build the eight trigrams and sixty-four hexagrams in the I-Ching. The hexagrams are created from all the possible combinations of the eight trigrams. Consulting the I-Ching is done in one of two ways. The most common way to generate a hexagram is by the random tossing of three coins while thinking of the question about which one wishes to gain knowledge. The second method for generating a hexagram is to divide fifty sticks (commonly yarrow sticks) into random piles which eventually form the hexagram. Whether using sticks or coins, the process is similar. Because coins are the easiest, they are most often used. Three coins are tossed, and it is noted if they fall with heads or tails facing upward. This pattern generates either a broken or a straight line. The coins are tossed a total of six times, and starting with the bottom line, two trigrams are built. A hexagram is composed of two trigrams; the first three lines form the lower one, and the second three throws form the top. The resulting trigrams are then correlated with a chart which is found in the back of most I-Ching books. This chart assists you to find the hexagram (by number) which your throws indicate is the advice of the oracle.

Many people who have consulted the I-Ching have found that it seems to develop a personality. This personality varies depending on the interpretation (book) which one is reading, but generally one begins to feel that a wise friend is sharing the counsel of many years. Answers are sometimes humorous, while at other times the I-Ching can even seem testy, advising one that it has already given advice on a particular subject and that one has but to heed it. It is, however, at most times a gentle friend to whom one can turn when direction is needed.

The new women's I-Ching. When reading I-Ching, the book/interpretation that one is using can have a profound effect on the advice which one receives. Each book contains its own interpretation of the sixty-four hexagrams, and, depending on the author's understanding of Chinese culture and personal point of view, the interpretations may vary widely.

Some of the most traditional I-Ching interpretations are literally translations of the original written Chinese text. In common use is the Wilhelm/Baynes edition* (Bollingen Foundation). There is a beauty and a purity to this book, but, as also discussed earlier, the social and political definitions in this book is not always affirming of women's experience. Recently, several New Age I-Chings have appeared. Based on the original meanings of the hexagrams, the text is paraphrased into more common word usage and to reflect values which are more consistent with the Aquarian ideology. Although these books are easier to read, understand, and most times agree with, they do occasionally contain a subtle sexism within their wording and images.

In 1985, the first women's I-Ching, *The Kwan Yin Book of Changes* * was published by Llewellyn Press. Diane Stein, a veteran of the women's spiritual movement, undertook the task of reclaiming the I-Ching into a document which was woman-oriented. Stein's I-Ching was closely followed by Barbara Walker's *The I-Ching of the Goddess,* * published in 1986. The ability to read an I-Ching which did not simultaneously require a wariness about the material has brought the I-Ching truly into the realm of feminist spirituality. The images of these I-Chings are of the matriarchy, the Goddess, the cycles of the year, and sisterhood. They bring the I-Ching to women in a way which speaks to them in their own words and validates their perceptions of the universe.

These books have, perhaps for the first time, claimed a written I-Ching for women. Returning the I-Ching to its matriarchal origins makes it an effective divinatory tool for the feminist seeker. As the women of spirit incorporate these new women's I-Chings into their complement of divinatory systems, the I-Ching will undoubtedly become one of the favorites of the women's spiritual community.

Dowsing

General information about dowsing. Perhaps the most obviously psychokinetic divinatory system being used by feminist Witches today is dowsing. Dowsing is the "quick fix" of divinatory arts. If one needs information and does not have time for a tarot reading or I-Ching, the pendulum stands ready to provide practically instant information about a question or an issue. This is not to say that dowsing is not taken seriously. Although held suspect by some and riding perilously close to the line of the true occult, dowsing is being used by women of spirit in many creative and useful ways.

Dowsing involves using a stick, metal rod, or pendulum to find information. Many people are familiar with water witching or dowsing for water. Using dowsing rods to locate underground water is a practice that is used by plumbers and dowsers even in conservative, rural communities. The tools of dowsing can range from the simple to the decorative and complex. Pendulums can be made from car keys or gem stones. Dowsing rods can be made of copper, heavy gauge plastic, a tree branch, or a coat hanger, and all can be equally effective. The simpler of these can be made at any moment. This simplicity makes dowsing an accessible divinatory system able to answer yes/no questions and to provide information quickly, often using materials on hand at the time.

Dowsing is used among women of spirit in many ways. Some carry pendulums with them in a pocket or bag. These can be consulted at any time when information is needed. Lost on the highway? Need to know what herbal preparation to take? Forgot your favorite recipe? The pocket pendulum can assist you with rapid answers. Pendulums and dowsing rods are also being used seriously by healing practitioners. These healers believe that information about the health of a person can be gained by use of pendulum, and that blockages in an aura can be detected with dowsing rods. Even the psychically impaired can use dowsing with great success. If one is not in touch with her intuitive feelings or is hesitant about discovering them, dowsing can be an excellent way to gradually awaken and confirm them. One caution about dowsing, however; dowsing rods and pendulums can be easily influenced both by psychic intention and by conscious direction. A pendulum or dowsing rod in the hands of an unethical person can become a power tool which confirms their wishes by simply intentionally moving the tool.

What can one expect when dowsing? A pendulum is most often used when one seeks answers to yes/no questions. The first time a pendulum is used, it is held over the palm and asked to indicate what movement it will make for "yes;" after being stilled, it is then asked what movement it will make for "no." The pendulum will usually begin to move in two distinct directions within a few moments. Often it moves in a circular fashion or back and forth. These movements by the pendulum indicate an affirmative or negative response and can then be used to answer a specific question.

Dowsing rods come in different types, and each is useful for various sorts of divination. A forked stick, a long supple branch, a slender metal rod, or two flexible pieces of plastic bound together at one end can be used for divining information about energy fields. These are the traditional tools for dowsing for water, and they are being used in the women's community both for this purpose and for finding the natural lines of energy in the earth (ley lines) and for finding energy centers for ritual. Dowsing rods are most often used when the information which one is seeking is contained in a horizontal structure such as the earth or floors. For information contained in a vertical plane, bent dowsing rods (one of which is held in each hand) are used. The rods usually consist of slender pieces of metal bent at a 90-degree angle with some type of handles which allow the rods to swing freely in an unrestricted arc. The metal can range from copper (thought to be a good conductor of the subtle energy fields sought in dowsing) to average closet-variety coat hangers. These types of dowsing rods can be used to dowse auras by walking toward a person or object and monitoring when the rods begin to open. The opening of the rods indicates contact with an energy field or any other vertical energy source.

Although feminists are using dowsing, there is very little information about dowsing that is woman-oriented. Good information about dowsing is available from the American Society of Dowsers.* The Society seemingly does not acknowledge any of the more metaphysical uses of dowsing, but does provide useful information about the "how to" of the art of dowsing.

Runes

General information about runes There are two common uses of runes within the women's community. One is for divination and the other is as an actual alphabet. Runes can be any of several sets of characters used by the ancient Germanic or Scandinavian peoples.

During the burning times, the spell books and journals of Witches (called Books of Shadows) are thought to have been kept in runic alphabets in order to protect the information from discovery. This has led to the definition of runes as a mystical alphabet having mysterious powers. Feminist Witches are using runic alphabets to write spells and to record information in their own Books of Shadows. This is done not so much to keep the information secret as it is to assure that the focused energy which is required to write in runes goes into their magical work.

What can one expect when using runes? Currently, divination with runes is popular within the mainstream New Age community. This use of runes is another psychokinetic divinatory form. The tools of runic divination include a bag of tiles, stones or wood pieces with a different runic symbol on each and a book of interpretations of the symbols. The tiles are shaken, and one is picked upon which the reading is based. The interpretations in *The Book of Runes,** by Ralph Blum, are shorter than the hexagrams of the I-Ching and, in general, have a more New Age focus which makes the use of this system both quicker and clearer then the traditional I-Ching. Also, like the I-Ching, runes depend largely on the intuitive ability of the reader. The interpretations rely on the individual consulting the runes to use their intuition to understand the advice of the runes.

The women's community is now exploring runes. Shekhinah Mountainwater has developed a set of womanrunes which bring runes into a form which can be used by women of spirit without conflict and there are other more experimental runic systems also being used by women. Runes have not been totally reclaimed by women of spirit as yet, but it seems likely that many woman-oriented runic systems will shortly join the variety of women's divinatory tools available. It remains to be seen if runic divination will become popular with women Witches; if the ingenuity with which previous divinatory systems have been reclaimed is applied to runes, then we can soon look forward to another woman-centered source of insight.

Ouija

General information about Ouija. Ouija is another psychokinetic divinatory tool which also utilizes a form of mediumship. Many women of spirit feel that the use of a Ouija board goes over the line into the true occult; as such, it is not popular. The information gained through the board is often thought to be unreliable, and the potential for the process to be manipulated looms large in the women's spiritual community's evaluation of this tool. The directness of the answers, be they right or wrong, is very different from the gentle guideposts of the tarot and the I-Ching and requires little insight by the individual seeking information. Ouija puts responsibililty on the individual(s) using the board more than other forms of psychokinetic divination discussed earlier. This is primarily because it is a blended system including psychokinetic and psychic skills. The use of psychic-based divinatory systems and attitudes toward them are discussed more extensively in the next section.

Although held suspect by many, Ouija does seem to awaken and validate latent psychic abilities. Individuals who are intuitive often begin to anticipate the responses of the board which can lead to recognition of mediumship skills. This causes one to wonder if the bad reputation of Ouija is not based, at least in part, on the reaction of psychic individuals to using the board. These individuals are often uncomfortable because they know the answer before it is finished and assume that they are influencing the outcome.

What to expect when consulting Ouija. Ouija involves the use of a board and a planchette. The planchette is a small, heart shaped plastic piece with a clear portion in the center. The board generally has the letters of the alphabet, numbers (zero though nine), and the words "yes," "no," and "good-bye" printed on its surface. In order to use the Ouija board, usually two individuals (occasionally one) place their hands (or their fingertips) on the planchette.

Questions are asked, and the kinetic energy of the individuals moves the planchette (assumingly without conscious intention) to spell out letters or identify the numbers/words which answer the inquiries. This can be a time-consuming process, the results of which are often unclear.

Ouija can be an informative tool which awakens psychic ability, or it can be an incredible hoax. If you decide to use Ouija as a divinatory system, choose your partners with care, and use your intuitive skills in evaluating any information which you receive.

■ *Psychic-based Intuition*

Like Ouija, the use of most psychic-based divination is approached with caution by the women's spiritual community. Psychic-based divination has long been in the realm of the true occult. Women who choose to practice the psychic-based divinatory arts (crystal gazing/scrying, aura readings, consulting spirit guides, interpreting dreams, or mediumship/channelling) may risk being judged by members of the spiritual women's community as at worst, a charlatan, or at best, a talented anachronism.

At the same time, most members of the women's community wish desperately to develop their psychic skills. Many women are cautiously experimenting with these divinatory arts which are the legacy of the spiritual divination of the matriarchy. It is also true, however, that feminist spiritualists are often reluctant to speak of their use of psychic-based divination or to credit the source of information gained through these methods.

This hesitancy is often found when attempting to discuss any revelatory experience, both inside and outside the women's community. Women who receive knowledge and direction from non-rational, intuitive sources often find it difficult to convey this information in any meaningful way to others. Knowledge gained through psychic-based divination often comes in symbols or concepts which are valid to that individual but which are difficult to translate to another person. If an individual is searching for direction and, suddenly, seemingly from out of nowhere, a bird crosses her path, it may symbolically indicate to her which direction to pursue. To attempt to communicate this experience to another may prove futile unless they share a similar symbolic language.

The Hazards of Psychic-based Divination

This same process of interpretation of symbols by the person who is practicing psychic-based divination is one of the greatest hazards of this type of divination. Because "feminist psychic" is almost a contradiction in terms, many of the people who are comfortable practicing psychic-based divination do not identify as feminists, as Witches, or even as members of any alternative religion. This does not seem to stop many women's desire to have their intuition confirmed or directions pointed by a "real psychic." So feminists are quietly consulting psychics, many of whom have a strong traditional belief system.

Anyone seeking a psychic counselor or reader should remember that the interpretation of the symbols or concepts that the psychic receives are filtered through the consciousness of the reader. This means that although the psychic may receive symbols or concepts which are valid to you and your life, the interpretation may be skewed by her own belief structure. Examples of common types of misinterpretation may include advising that you will meet the "right man" and get married when you have no intention or inclination to do so, insisting to an identifiable lesbian that she was a man in her past life and that any current identity problems stem from that source, encouragement to pray and/or assumptions that you will wish to honor traditional religions, and encouraging traditional relationship choices.

Psychic-based Divination among Women of Spirit

It has taken a full ten years for many members of the women's spiritual community to become comfortable with the use of psychic- based divination, and some are not yet comfortable with these practices. Dreams, reading auras, and contact with spirit guides are gaining acceptance and are being practiced and developed within women's circles. These are considered advanced work by many and not to be taken lightly. Use of any of these divinatory arts requires personal responsibility on the part of the reader, and, communication of information gained through these sources is often difficult. Regardless of the stigma attached to psychic-based divination, women of spirit are pursuing these systems with interest and integrity.

Dreams

Perhaps the most commonly accepted form of psychic communication in the women's spiritual community is dreaming. The use of dreams to access psychic information does not require any special tools. Since most people dream and since individuals are thought to have little control over the content of their dreams, gaining symbolic information through dreams is not considered to be unusual. Feminist spiritualists seek to interpret dream symbolism in a context affirming to women's experience. The patriarchal legacy of dream interpretation is most often held as invalid. Over-the-counter dream books are considered useless, Freudian analysis is definitely out, and Jungian analysis is suspect.

How women interpret dreams and what they do with the information gained through dreams has not, as yet, developed into any recognized system. Meeting with dream groups, dream circles, and keeping dream journals are not uncommon practices in the feminist community. Even women who are not strongly identified with any other spiritual activity may keep a dream journal or participate with a dream group. However, dream interpretation has in no way become a formalized process within the women's spiritual community. The responses of the dreamer to the symbols of the dream are what is held as valid. Symbolism is not expected to be consistent from individual to individual. Exploring a house with many rooms may be a symbol of personal growth for one woman, for another it may mean discovering hidden parts of herself, while for a third it may indicate a more complex job is upcoming. The responsibility for interpreting and acting on information gained through dreams is on the individual dreamer. For some women the information gained through dreams is a major source of direction for action in their lives, while for others it may be a way to uncover their intuitive selves.

Auras

It is not unusual to hear members of the larger women's community speak of auras. The word aura is in common use, and the concept of auras is generally accepted by women of spirit. The aura is thought to be a body of energy which surrounds the physical body and which is visible to a majority of individuals if they know how to look for it.

Like dreams, there are no particular tools that are thought to be needed to gain information about auras. Reading the aura is based on psychically and rationally analyzing the shapes, colors and patterns of a person's aura and interpreting them. Again, how these symbols are interpreted is a very individual process. Feminist spiritualists are suspicious of any hard and fast definition of what a particular color or shape means when it is in an aura. For one woman, it may mean that she is experiencing anger, while for another it may mean intense sexual energy. Having one's aura read can provide many different types of information. The colors and shapes of an aura can indicate one's general health and emotional state. Therefore, the aura can be used as a diagnostic tool in healing work. Many women working in healing believe that the aura will show the beginnings of disease or illness before it appears on the physical plane.

Diane Mariechild's *Mother Wit* includes a chapter on learning to work with auras, and Kay Gardner, feminist singer, composer, and musician, has conducted aura sensing workshops attended by hundreds of women over the past decade. Kay is respected in the women's community both for her music and for her ability to encourage women to experiment with their visual psychic abilities. She and other women of spirit have been active in teaching women both how to see and sense auras.

It is often difficult to find a feminist aura reader, but many mainstream psychics can and do give aura readings. If you choose to have your aura read by a psychic, be she feminist or not, the same advice as given about general psychic-based divination still applies. Be cautious of how the colors and patterns of your aura are interpreted, and use your intuition to check the validity of both the reader and the reading.

Spirit Guides

In almost all spiritual traditions, there is a concept of communication and/or contact with progressed, non-form beings. These can range from the plant divas of the Indian tradition to the guardian angels of Christianity. Within the women's community these non-form friends are called spirit guides and are thought to be a generally reliable source of non-rational, psychic-based information. The definitions of spirit guides and their supposed place in feminist cosmology vary widely. Some women of spirit believe that spirit guides are a part of the higher self of an individual. Others think that spirit guides are actually separate, non-form entities who have taken an interest in an individual woman or who have agreed to assist her with her sojourn on the Earth plane. Although consensus has not been reached about the exact function or place of residence of one's guides, cultivation of spirit guides is generally accepted in the women's spiritual community.

Most feminist spiritualists acknowledge that some force, seemingly beyond themselves, often offers information or advice. The "little voices" commonly heard or experienced among women who pursue their spiritual options will often times be recognized easily as spirit guides when that term is introduced. Spirit guides are most often personified as individual beings, each believed to have certain areas of expertise or knowledge. Within some traditional occult circles, spirit guides come in proscriptive personality types. The doctor/teacher, the joy guide, the Indian (Native American) guide, and a host of others (up to seven per person) comprise a traditional contingent of spirit guides. As in most areas of spiritual endeavor, feminists are far more open, believing that one can have any number of spirit guides and that they do not come in ready-made sets.

For women who are not aware of their inner voices, identifying and contacting spirit guides is a skill that can be learned. Diane Mariechild has exercises for contacting spirit guides in *Mother Wit* as does Hallie Inglehart in *Womanspirit*. Generally, these exercises involve either meditation on meeting one's spirit guide and receiving information from them or having actual conversations with a spirit guide assuming that eventually one (or more) will answer.

The idea of spirit guides is one which many women of spirit find comforting. Spiritual women can, at times, feel isolated from spiritual contact as they go about their daily lives. Spirit guides offer a source of constant reinforcement and support for a spiritual focus in all activities of life. Although considered escapist by some, spirit guides enjoy quiet acceptance by many members of the women's spiritual community.

Mediumship or Channelling

Mediumship and its modern cousin, "channelling," are the traditional pinnacles of psychic-based divination. They provide direct access to information from an intuitive source. Mediumship/channelling requires no identifiable stimulus as in dreams or aura reading. Although within the matriarchy, prophesy (which is close kin to mediumship/channelling) was one of the most highly practiced forms of divination, mediumship/channelling has met with marginal acceptance by women of spirit.

Strong prohibitions about the use of mediumship/channelling arose after traditional religions began to have power, and many of these prohibitions still color perceptions among woman of spirit. Prophesy, long considered primarily a women's skill, was replaced in many traditional religions by the role of the priest/rabbi as intercessor and interpreter of the will of a deity. Taboos which prohibited the use of prophesy can still be found in the Bible. In addition to this cultural prohibition against the use of prophesy, we have all been well schooled about the potential hazards of consulting mediums. We have been taught that mediums, and now channelers, are unreliable and out to bilk unsuspecting victims into turning over their worldly goods in thankfulness for the information and direction which the medium provides. Other stereotypes about mediums are that they are traditionally thought to have an unhealthy association with the dead and, in many cases, to have gained their skill through some unsavory occult means.

In the women's spiritual community, these same attitudes are not uncommon. It is important to many women of spirit that their spiritual activities are not considered "too far out," and mediumship/channelling is one of the activities which is often considered to be truly over the line of common sense. The actual potential of a medium to misinterpret or to manipulate information to suit their interests is too great for many women of spirit to feel very comfortable. So long the bastion of the traditional occult and charlatan alike, the use of mediumship/channelling requires our socialization about mediums/channellers and our motivation for seeking information through them be re-evaluated. Some spiritual women who seek out a medium/channeller for guidance have found they have grown from this experience. However, to consult a medium/channeller for daily direction and to give over personal power are very different matters. Women of spirit are exploring mediumship/channelling with hesitation. They are, with extreme caution, consulting traditional mediums/channellers and subjecting the information gained though these encounters to close scrutiny. Very few spiritual feminists attend seances or accept practices such as table tapping, direct communication with the dead, or apport manifestation (producing material objects allegedly from some cosmic source).

This is not to say that there is a total lack of acceptance or interest in mediumship/channelling in the women's spiritual community. Some women feel that, like many of the other spiritual traditions of the matriarchy, mediumship/channelling has been improperly maligned and it may be that this is yet another divinatory system which women will yet reclaim.

Crystal Gazing or Scrying

Crystal gazing or scrying is the use of a crystal, dark mirror, polished obsidian stone, or still water as a focus point to alter one's perceptions and to allow a free flow of psychic information. This is the only form of psychic-based divination used in the women's community which requires a tool. The traditional crystal ball is the most well known tool of this divinatory art. Before proceding any further, it will probably be useful to separate the use of natural crystal points from crystal gazing or scrying. The use of various crystals, particularly quartz crystals, in healing work and in channelling energy is currently one of the most popular areas of study within both the mainstream New Age community and women's spiritual circles. Natural quartz crystals are considered to be excellent conductors of the more subtle energy forces used in healing work and in channelling directed energy. New Age practitioners of all types are attempting to define and refine the use of crystals as energy conductors and as healing tools.

This use of natural crystal is quite a bit different from the use of crystal for divination. Crystal divination is most often not done with natural crystal simply because true crystal is very costly. Pure quartz crystal balls are available, but the expense of purchasing crystal can range from about sixty dollars for a two-inch ball to several thousand dollars for a five-inch ball. Because this expense is prohibitive for most would-be scryers, quartz crystal balls are seldom used. Instead, women of spirit tend to use a range of alternative scrying tools.

One substitute for the crystal ball is leaded crystal available in many New Age and occult bookstores and even in mainstream department stores. Leaded crystal has the clarity and many of the qualities of true crystal. It is less expensive and, for many scryers, equally effective. A dark mirror (a mirror which is tinted gray or black) or a piece of polished obsidian can also be effective scrying tools. Dark mirrors can often be found in a mirror or glass store, and polished obsidian is available at special request from most rock or lapidary shops. The expense for either of these tools is generally in the twenty-to-fifty-dollar range depending on size and quality. For those who want to try scrying on an extremely low budget, a simple dark bowl of water or a clear still pool can achieve the same result.

Scrying involves focusing both visual and psychic energy on one of the tools above to create an altered state in which intuitive information can be gained. Women who are visually-oriented seem to find this type of divination is particularly effective as the information gained through scrying is generally presented in visual images. As with any of the psychic-based divinatory systems, the interpretation of the symbols and images gained through scrying is what the advice or action is based upon, and one should be careful to ensure that the symbols are interpreted in a way which affirms women's experience.

Scrying is not often practiced within the women's spiritual community. In fact, it is so little known that many women of spirit do not even know the definition of the term scrying. Because of this, there is no information from a feminist basis available on scrying. It remains to be seen what level of acceptance scrying will have within the women's spiritual community until its use is more well known. Interestingly, scrying is also rare among mainstream psychics. The traditional psychic with the crystal ball is an image that is difficult for even mainstream occultists to feel comfortable with. Therefore, finding anyone who can assist you with a reading based on scrying is usually not an option. Interest in scrying may be an outgrowth of the crystal study which is currently being pursued in the women's community and the

New Age community at large, but until then, scrying remains an all but forgotten form of psychic-based divination.

■ Scientific-based Divination

The decision to include scientific-based systems in a chapter on divination is one which could be disputed. For many, the true definition of divination includes a presumption that the source of the information gained is primarily psychic and that it does not have a scientific base as do astrology, numerology, or other methods for seeking information. Some practitioners of these scientific arts would argue that they do, indeed, include psychic skills in the interpretation of a chart or other data, while other practitioners argue that psychic ability has nothing to do with the information acquired. Still others would argue that neither astrology nor numerology has any basis in true science.

In most of the divinatory arts discussed thus far, the information used to give direction to a seeker is gained from a source that is difficult to pinpoint as the actual, finite origin of that knowledge. In scientific-based divination, this is not the case. In astrology, numerology, or graphology, the formula that is used to construct and identify data, if done correctly, is totally replicable by another practitioner. Also unlike the other divinatory systems discussed thus far, scientific-based systems enjoyed more acceptance by the power structure in the centuries of rational thought. Because of this, most scientific-based systems bring with them hundreds of years of traditional interpretations. When kinetic and psychic-based divination were forced underground because of social and religious stigma, scientific divinatory methods held a tentative acceptance even in patriarchal culture. As a consequence, there is a legacy of interpretation of the data generated by scientific disciplines. These traditional interpretations can be memorized or referenced as a basis for the advice given to a seeker.

So how does knowledge gained from a psychic source factor into science-based divination? After constructing a chart or analyzing graphic or numerological data, the interpretation of the information gathered from these sources is subject to the translation of the practitioner. Many of these practitioners credit both an intuitive and a rational basis for this translation. Interpretation of an astrological chart may, for example, include a blending of information about a planet and the house in which that planet falls. Although this information can be found in a rational form in astrological books, many practitioners rely on a psychic basis to synthesize the effects of these two factors and how they will manifest as the forms and circumstances of a person's life. This introduces into these potentially rational and scientific systems a psychic element which some believe moves them into the realm of divination.

If you are considering seeking assistance in analyzing astrological, numerological, or graphological data, it may be useful for you to identify whether the practitioner that you are consulting uses a psychic or a rational basis. Because of the finite existence of data in scientific-based divination, it has potentially fewer hazards than many of the other divinatory systems discussed thus far. If you question the information that you receive from one astrologer or numerologist, simply take your chart or numerological data to another for a second opinion. If you find that the practitioner that you are consulting relies strongly on a psychic basis for translating the knowledge contained in your chart or other data, then the same cautions apply as those discussed in psychic-based divination. If, on the other hand, a practitioner uses only scientific facts for accessing the information, be cautious of potential patriarchal bias.

Scientific-based Divination among Women of Spirit

Because many women of spirit approach divination in an attempt to free themselves from the bounds of rational thought, divinatory systems which have a rational basis are not, with the exception of astrology, in common use by these women. Apparently, trying to find intuitive information through a rational means is not a comfortable choice. Women, in general, have been socialized to believe that they are not good at the various skills that scientific-based divination require. Many women have "math anxiety" and, when faced with calculating the figures required to generate astrological charts or numerological analyses they may be unsure of their ability. In almost every community, however, there are women who are exceptions. Although numerologists are few in women's circles, astrologers are quite common. Feminist astrologers comprise a significant component of the innovative thinkers in astrology today. Within the women's community itself, astrology is the only scientific divination method in prevalent use. There is, therefore, little woman-centered information available about numerology or graphology; as a result of this, the only scientific method that will be discussed in this section is astrology.

General information about astrology.   Astrology has been used for generations in societies which remained close to their matriarchal origins. In
India, a country where thousands of Goddesses are worshipped even
today, astrological charts are constructed for babies at birth and are
consulted before any major life choices are made. Many astrologers believe that the current astrological system is but a pale reflection of complex astrologies that existed in the past. For example, there are rem-
nants of a thirteen-sign zodiac, following the thirteen lunar months in a
year and containing, some say, the sign Arachne, whose symbol was a
spider or a spinner. Since spinning was considered a woman's art, in
virtually all matriarchal cultures it comes as no surprise that Arachne
was considered a woman-centered sign. This is only one example of
the many woman-affirming aspects of astrology which were lost or replaced over the centuries.

Most women have been led to believe that astrology is extremely
complicated, requiring years of study and an ability to do advanced
math. Astrology, however, can be pursued on many levels. It can be an
easily accessible source of self knowledge or an intense scientific study,
depending on how one approaches it. The first step in generating data
in astrology is the construction of a chart, which requires information
on the time, date, and place of your birth. The more accurate this information is, the more accurate your chart and the insights gained from it
will be. These statistics are used to determine where the planets were
at the moment that you were born and to place them in houses (the
twelve pie-shaped pieces that comprise a chart). With this information
you have several choices as to how to gain knowledge about yourself
through astrology.

Probably the simplest choice is to consult a professional astrologer.
In most communities, there is probably a woman who can construct
and interpret your chart for you. In many women's communities, there
may be someone who is quietly doing charts for her friends and family,
and you simply need to ask if anyone knows of someone who does
charts. If you can't find or don't have access to a woman-identified
astrologer, you can simply look up astrologers in the phone book in
larger cities; also try checking at a New Age or occult bookstore for
postings of local astrologers. Be sure to ascertain what the astrologer
uses as a basis for chart interpretation, and be careful of the possible
non-feminist interpretations of mainstream astrologers. Because of the
patriarchal legacy of astrology there are many areas in which one can

receive an unnecessarily negative or biased reading based on concepts which are not accepted by feminist astrologers.

One of the major reasons why many women choose not to pursue astrology is financial. The average cost of having a chart constructed and interpreted can range from $20 to $300, depending on where you live and who you choose. A $50-$75 fee will probably get you as good a reading as the more expensive ones. Having your chart done by someone who specializes in constructing and interpreting charts is a valid choice when you want information quickly and are not interested or do not have the time to educate yourself about astrology.

If you are interested in learning about astrology but the math required is more than you care to tackle, then computerized astrology may be an answer for you. Thanks to the computer age, there are several automated options available to the would-be astrologer. Because astrology has a scientific basis, the mathematical information needed to construct a chart can be programmed into a computer. If you have a personal computer, astrological programs are available for most home computer systems. These programs take the data of the person for whom you are constructing a chart and, in moments, provide a printout. For those not lucky enough to have access to a personal computer, computerized chart services provide the same information at a rapid speed and low cost. Accurate computerized charts can be obtained for little money and are generally returned in under two weeks. Astro-Computing Services, P.O. Box 16430, San Diego, CA 92116, for example, provides excellent charts for only a few dollars.

Once you have a printout, whether it was done on your home computer or purchased from a chart service, the interpretation is then up to you. There are many good books on astrological interpretation that can assist in understanding the knowledge hidden in a chart. *The Only Way to Learn Astrology, Volume I*, by Marion March and Joan McEvers is an excellent book for beginners in astrological interpretations. It does contain some traditional interpretations, but the basic information about chart interpretation is very clear and readable. Many women who believed that astrology was beyond them have found that, with a little reading and practice, they can interpret a chart with ease.

Another choice for those who are truly interested in pursuing all the nuances of astrology is to learn to construct and interpret charts yourself. Classes are often offered by knowledgeable astrologers and even through community adult education programs. These classes can teach you the basics of both chart construction and astrological interpretation.

What can one expect from an astrological reading? Many people consider astrology to be a form of divination because the information gained from astrological interpretations is so similar to that which is gained through other forms of divination. The insights acquired through an understanding of one's chart can be surprisingly comprehensive. Astrological interpretation includes within its purview data about most areas of life: personality, relationships, family, friends, career, money, business, travel, interests, quirks, spirituality, and many others. Some consider an astrological chart to be a blueprint detailing the assets and liabilities with which one entered this life. It can show where there may be challenges, when they might occur, and what one might want to consider doing in response to them. What seems most surprising to many women who have their charts read is the startling accuracy with which their charts fit their personalities and life circumstances. Because many of us have a passing knowledge of sun sign astrology and because we assume it to be the sum and total of astrological analysis, the information contained in a total chart is often profound and unexpected.

An interesting difference between astrology and the psychic and kinetic divinatory systems discussed earlier is the relationship of astrology to time. Psychic- and kinetic-based divination tend to freeze a moment in time (past, present, or future) while astrology acknowledges the movement of the planets through time and their varying effects on an individual. So although having your chart read can give specific information about a current issue, it can also predict times of triumph or stress in the future or past. Once constructed, a chart can be consulted again and again to find information about your relationship to the cosmos.

Attitudes of the women's community toward astrology. Astrology enjoys a tentative acceptance in the women's community. Talk of astrology can receive any number of responses from humorous acceptance to serious dialogue. Most women know their sun signs and many know their moon and ascendant (rising) signs. Astrology can often generate table talk over dinner or party conversation even among those who seem to have little other interest in spiritual activities.

Serious feminist astrologers are currently reclaiming astrological interpretations which reflect values affirming to women's reality. Traditional astrological interpretations which assign a female and a male (passive and dominant) nature to planets and to qualities within a chart are being reinterpreted to reflect the more inclusive concepts about sex and sexuality believed by many feminists. In *God Herself: The Feminine Roots of Astrology*, Geraldine Thorsten traces the woman-centered and matriarchal origins of astrology and places them in a perspective which is at one with the experience of women today. This book is good reading for women simply interested in matriarchal thought and for astrologers as well. However, there are also books like *Woman's Astrology* by Tiffany Holmes, which allegedly respond to women's charts but have nothing to do with the lives of women who are redefining their role in society.

Although there are many forms of divination which have not been discussed in this chapter, these are the most common forms in practice within the women's spiritual community. Since the early seventies, divination has been a major focus of creative energy. Women of spirit have developed their own tarots and I-Chings; they are reclaiming knowledge of psychic divination systems and are creating astrologies which reflect women's experience. Many believe this is only the beginning of a store of knowledge that will grow along with the women's spiritual community. Divination is valued in this community for the direction and advice it has provided to many, but primarily divination is and will remain a major tool for women of spirit to find and reconnect with the wisdom of the Goddess within themselves.

■ Resources

Tarot

Tarot Network News, 2860 California Street, San Francisco, CA 94115.

The Winged Chariot, c/o MoonStar Enterprises, P.O. Box 8458, San Diego, CA 92102.

Z. Budapest, *The Holy Book of Women's Mysteries*. Berkeley, CA: Wingbow Press, 1989.

Gail Fairfield, *Choice Centered Tarot*. Seattle, WA: Choices, 1984.

Sally Gearhart, *A Feminist Tarot*. Watertown, MA: Persephone Press, 1977.

Vicki Noble, *Motherpeace: A Way to the Goddess through Myth, Art and Tarot*. San Francisco: Harper and Row, 1983.

Billie Potts, *A New Women's Tarot*. Woodstock, NY: Elf and Dragons Press, 1978.

Barbara G. Walker, *The Secrets of the Tarot: Origins, History, and Symbolism*. San Francisco: Harper and Row, 1984.

I-Ching

Diane Stein, *The Kwan Yin Book of Changes*. St. Paul, MN: Llewellyn Publications, 1985.
Barbara G. Walker, *The I-Ching of the Goddess*. San Francisco: Harper and Row, 1986.
Wilhelm/Baynes, *I-Ching*. Princeton, NJ: Princeton University Press, 1981.
R. L. Wing, *The I-Ching Workbook*. Garden City, NY: Doubleday & Company, 1979.

Dowsing

American Society of Dowsers, Danville, VT 05828.

Psychic Development

Hallie Inglehart, *Womanspirit*. San Francisco: Harper and Row, 1983.
Diane Mariechild, *Mother Wit*. Trumansburg, NY: The Crossing Press, 1981.

Runes

Ralph Blum, *The Book of Runes*. New York: St. Martin's Press, 1982.
Shekhinah Mountainwater, *Womanrunes* (runeset). P.O. Box 2991, Santa Cruz, CA 95062.

Astrology

Astro-Computing Services, P.O. Box 16430, San Diego, CA 92116.
Marion D. March and Joan McEvers, *The Only Way to Learn Astrology, Volume I*. San Diego: Astro-Computing Services, 1980.
Derek and Julia Parker, *The Compleat Astrologer*. New York: Bantam Books, 1975.
Geraldine Thorsten, *God Herself: The Feminine Roots of Astrology*. New York: Avon, 1980.

CHAPTER **6**

Women's Spiritual and Pagan Cultures

In our complex world it is difficult to say exactly what makes up a culture. When most people speak of a culture, they are attempting to define actions, beliefs, and activities that differentiate one group of people from another. Using this definition, it becomes clear that since the sixties both the women's movement and the Pagan movement have been forming cultures. Underground societies are growing out of the ideology and thealogy of women's spirituality and mainstream Paganism. These cultures have emerging traditions and philosophies which are separate and different from the larger norm as well as from each other. In developing woman-centered spirituality, a great deal of information has been generated and collected which is helping to create a woman-centered culture. Many women are anxious to learn about feminist religion, and much of the activity in the women's spiritual community today includes developing ways to pass on this knowledge.

One of the first activities of any developing culture is to begin its own network of communication. Journals and newspapers are the primary form of contact in both the women's spiritual community and within mainstream Paganism. Perhaps because many Pagans don't have access to others with whom they can hold dialogue or simply because Pagans as a group tend to read more than the average American, journals and newspapers are both a primary means of communication and a major source of contact. It is in these publications that discussion takes place. Exploration of ideas, sharing of traditions, and philosophical disagreements often occur in print media. You may want to "shop" among the newsletters, papers, journals, and other periodicals since each reflects a different approach and philosophy.

Women's spiritual and Pagan publications vary widely in quality and content. Some of these publications are excellent, while others are poorly produced and edited by folks who, one suspects, did not excel in traditional scholastic efforts. A few publications thrive on controversy while others shy away from it and attempt to convey a spirit of unity. Some are very proscriptive and claim to know the "secrets" for the true practice of the Craft, while others are more open to various viewpoints. Unfortunately, some of the people and groups who choose to publish papers and journals seem to have a limited understanding of the Craft, and their publications range from the trite to the absurd. However, a majority of the publishers are seriously involved in sharing the ideas, issues, and practices of women's spirituality and/or Paganism.

■ A Herstory of Women's Spiritual Periodicals

In the early seventies, women's spirituality was seeking a voice. In 1974, some women from a feminist magazine called *Country Women* attended a women's spirituality weekend in Oregon that Ruth and Jean Mountaingrove, along with Nellie Kaufer, sponsored. Intrigued by the experience, *Country Women* agreed to do an issue on the theme of women's spirituality. "Response to this issue, an intuition (after an I-Ching reading), and an envelope from a contributor led me [Jean] to think a continuing magazine was needed."[1] From this, *WomanSpirit** magazine was born. During much of its decade of publishing, it was the sole voice of communication for many spiritual women. At that time there was little printed information available in any form about women's spirituality, and *WomanSpirit* provided a valuable role in the formation, exploration, and dissemination of the ideas and philosophy of spiritual women. In 1984, *WomanSpirit* stopped publishing. The decision to cease publication was based on a variety of personal reasons, not the least of which were Ruth and Jean's primitive country living conditions which made publication difficult. Jean still continues to work with the legacy of *WomanSpirit*, offering back issues and working on an index of the articles and information that it contains.

Both during and after the publishing of *WomanSpirit*, other woman-oriented spiritual papers and journals began to appear. *Thesmophoria,*

Goddess Rising, Of a Like Mind, Woman of Power, and later *SageWoman* all began, and they continue to publish woman-oriented spiritual papers and journals. There is a wide range of style and content among these publications, reflecting the interests and ideas of their readers and editors, and they run from a glossy magazine format to newsprint tabloids.

Thesmophoria*

Thesmophoria is a small, but well done, newsletter published by the Susan B. Anthony Coven #1 in California. It is generally four typeset pages and is published quarterly. *Thesmophoria* has been publishing regularly since 1979, and it ranks as the oldest continuing women's spiritual perodical. It has often carried the description "the voice of the new feminist religion," and, at the time that it began publishing, it was the only paper which acknowledged women's spirituality as a religion. It frequently contains articles by Z. Budapest, who is the High Priestess of the Susan B. Anthony Coven and well known for her work in the Goddess movement. *Thesmophoria* includes articles, information, letters, poetry, reviews, ads, and a local calendar of events.

Goddess Rising*

Goddess Rising is a 12-page quarterly newspaper for womyn only. It is published by Goddess Rising Dianic Wicce Shop at each solstice and equinox. "The goals of this Journal are: to be a vehicle for womyn to share information, experiences and visions with a focus on womyn-identified, feminist spirituality, Dianic Wicce, positive magick, healing, ritual, rediscovering and reclaiming the Goddess within each of us—our power and strength as womyn. As such we ask that this paper be shared only with womyn."[2] This paper features articles and information celebrating a solely womyn-centered approach to Goddess religion. If you are interested in exploring women's spirituality in this form, *Goddess Rising* is a good resource. Please, however, respect the intent of this paper and share it only with womyn.

Of a Like Mind*

It seems a little strange to report about *Of a Like Mind* because to share information about the creation of this newspaper and network, I must tell a story about myself. To me it is a story of magic and of a young Witch receiving her vision. The story starts in 1975 when I lived in Louisville, Kentucky. Through interacting with my lesbian feminist community, I learned that some of the women in it considered themselves Witches. This was a thrill to me because I had for many years been trying to find information about how to use and control my psychic self. I began trying to educate myself about women's spirituality and how it was practiced. I soon learned, however, that most of the women I met who defined themselves as Witches could not answer my questions. It was, therefore, with great excitement that I heard of a conference called "Witches and Amazons" in Columbus, Ohio. A group of us decided to attend hoping that perhaps we would meet other women there who could give us direction in our spiritual quest. It was a wonderful and inspiring conference full of spiritual women and lectures about Amazons and the Craft. One of the speakers was Z. Budapest, who is a dynamic presenter. I was so motivated by Z.'s talk and by the conference that on the way home I announced to the women with whom I had attended the conference that if only I had some money, I would organize for the Goddess. At the time I thought that this was a pretty far-fetched idea, but when I returned home, the phone was ringing. It was my mother calling to tell me that my Grandmother had died and left me a small inheritance. With this I began my work organizing in the women's spiritual community.

Organizing was difficult in my Kentucky home. There was a small group of Goddess women which met together occasionally and attempted to provide support to each other around spiritual issues. However, most of the time, my talk of spirituality was met with either amazement or hostility. In spite of this, I began to work with these women organizing retreats, small gatherings, and seasonal celebrations. In time it became clear that Kentucky was not the place to sustain a concerted organizing effort. I felt isolated and lonely. I desperately wanted peers, other women who felt a passion for the Goddess.

So in 1982 I moved to Madison, Wisconsin, which has large women's and Pagan communities. I promised myself that I would never forget how it felt to be isolated as I had been in Kentucky. It seemed important to assist women in locating and identifying others in their area interested in spirituality. It also seemed that the best way to do this was through a newspaper and network. Unfortunately, I did not have the skills needed to publish a newspaper. I began to work my magic to draw to myself the perfect person to work with me. Shortly, I met

Lynnie Levy who is an amazing woman with all the skills needed to publish a newspaper, and for Hallows of 1983 the first issue of *Of a Like Mind* was published. Since then *Of a Like Mind* has grown to be one of the largest publications for spiritual women.

Of a Like Mind is a newspaper but it has an additional focus. It is the only women's publication which includes a network. Women who receive the newspaper also have the opportunity to join a network with a variety of services designed to assist spiritual women to make contact with each other. The *OALM* newspaper is published quarterly, and in addition to its articles, reviews, graphics, news, letters, commentary, and ads, it includes an extensive networking section which has announcements, events, listings of teachers, healers, groups, publications, stores, centers, artists/craftswomen and community contacts. "It is dedicated to bringing together ♀ following a positive path to spiritual growth. Its focus is on ♀'s spirituality, Goddess religions, Paganism and our earth connections from a feminist perspective."[3]

Woman of Power*

In 1985, women's spiritual publishing came of age with its first glossy magazine, *Woman of Power. Woman of Power* was the vision of Char McKee who called together a group of spiritual women in the Cambridge, Massachusetts, community to work together toward realizing this impressive undertaking. In the first years of the magazine, the dream was difficult to realize, and publication was sporadic as *Woman of Power* gained momentum. Now, however, *Woman of Power* is one of the most outstanding and dependable publications of the women's community, spiritual or otherwise.

"*Woman of Power* is a magazine of feminism, spirituality and politics."[4] It is published quarterly, and each issue has a specific theme. This is a beautiful magazine and a credit to the publishers' abilities of manifestation. This magazine includes more than information about women's spirituality. It also includes articles which are politically insightful, many of which have an underlying feminist and spiritual perspective.

SageWoman*

The newest addition to the growing number of spiritual women's journals is *SageWoman*. Begun in 1986, *SageWoman* is committed to following in the tradition of *WomanSpirit* and, in fact, it does resemble *WomanSpirit* in both format and content. "*SageWoman* magazine is a feminist, grass-roots quarterly centered on women's spirituality. . . . [*SageWoman* hopes] to provide a space for women of all ethnic and cultural backgrounds to share women's wisdom and women's mysteries. . . . [*SageWoman*] celebrates the Woman Shield: our sacred creativity, sacred intuition, introspection, earth and our physical bodies. *SageWoman* is dedicated to strengthening our inner visions and using those visions to transform our world."[5] *SageWoman* is an inspirational magazine filled with the dreams and visions of many women.

■ *Mainstream Pagan Papers and Journals*

The Pagan community is diverse and so are the number and variety of Pagan papers and journals. Similar to publications within the women's community, the scope, direction and production quality of Pagan papers and periodicals varies greatly. They range from poorly photocopied $8^1/2''$ by 11" sheets to well-organized and produced publications. The type of information contained in these publications may also vary greatly. Some publications are scholarly, serious, and focused, while others are light, cute, and do not seem to have a deep understanding of Paganism. The purpose of many mainstream publications is not quality but simply to serve as a source of communication among differing Pagan traditions and groups. Be sure to "shop" among mainstream Pagan publications. They range so widely that to be familiar with one Pagan publication gives little indication of what the total possibilities are.

There are differences between Pagan papers and journals and those publications which are intended for a women's audience. First, if you decide to read mainstream Pagan publications, it is important to remember that feminist Witches do not always receive blanket acceptance from all Pagans and that one should not always expect to find whole-hearted support for a woman-centered spirituality in all these publications. Additionally, they often have a God and Goddess focus rather than the Goddess orientation of the women's publications. This occasionally translates into outright sexism that can be offensive. Unfortunately, sometimes sexist statements that are published do reflect the opinion of the editor and/or editorial staff. However, more often, controversial material published about women is printed to provoke dialogue among readers and does not reflect the beliefs of the publisher. There are so many mainstream Pagan publications that if you find one offensive, there is no need to continue to read it. Requesting a sample issue is a good way to get an idea of the attitude of any specific publication towards women's issues.

There are many different ways to evaluate Pagan papers and journals. If you are interested in subscribing to a paper which has a very large circulation and a broad audience, *Circle Network News** is probably the paper which would best meet this criteria. If you are interested in dialogue, then you may want to consider *Harvest,* The Covenant of the Goddess Newsletter,** or *Panegyria** which often contain lively articles on topics under debate within the Pagan community. There are also newsletters of specific traditions, *The Georgian Newsletter** from the Georgian tradition, or *The Druids' Progress** from Ar nDraoícht Féin. Further, *Shaman's Drum,* Wildfire,** and *Moccasin Line** reflect Native American traditions, and *Earth First! The Radical Environmental Journal** occasionally carries articles about eco-spirituality.

Selecting Newspapers, Journals, and Newsletters

As discussed in Chapter Three, both women's spiritual and Pagan groups are continually changing. Because the Craft is traditionally an anarchistic religion, it often defies the structure required to support a regular publishing schedule. Many Craft publications seem to come and go within a fairly short period of time; because of this, many of the resources listed in this chapter may no longer be publishing by the time you read this.

When considering subscribing to publications, there are several factors one might want to consider, including the following:

–many of these publications have a specific focus. If you are looking for information specific to women's spirituality, for example, check the resource listing for those publications which are identified as specializing in women's issues.
–if you are looking for other Pagans or Witches in your area, then you may want to consider subscribing to a publication from your region or to one of the networking publications.
–you may want to consider subscribing to at least one publication which has ongoing dialogue. Subscribing to one of the papers which encourages an active exchange of ideas among diverse people is probably one of the best ways to stay informed.

If you would like information from any of the publications, be sure to enclose a large self-addressed, stamped envelope with your request.

Ordering a sample copy is probably the best way to evaluate which of the many papers offered is of the most interest to you. Prices for sample copies are included in the resource list when available.

If you are looking for more current information than is provided in this book, you may want to contact one of the networking organizations. In women's spirituality, the largest and oldest networking organization is *Of a Like Mind*. *Of a Like Mind* publishes a *Sourcebook* which lists many publications of interest to spiritual women. Circle* publishes the *Circle Guide to Pagan Resources* every few years which contains information about the mainstream Pagan community. In addition to listing publications, these directories also serve as guides to the teachers, healers, craftspersons, stores, and centers of this new society.

■ *Publications by and about Women Witches*

One of the questions I am most often asked is, "What books can I read to learn about women's spirituality?" This question comes both from women who are isolated and from women who read to acquire knowledge. In the seventies I was often at a loss about how to answer this question. Happily, this situation is being resolved. Many women who have an understanding of woman-centered spirituality are writing about the information they have gathered. The current choices of spiritual reading material have become both more specific and more plentiful. There are now many excellent books which have been written specifically about women's spirituality and others written from the perspective of more mainstream Pagans. The following books are the ones which I most often recommend. There are, of course, many other good books both about women's spirituality and about the Craft in general. This list includes my personal favorites and also the books which I consider the "basics" for an understanding of the Craft.

Books about the Craft

*Positive Magic: Occult Self-Help** by Marion Weinstein

This is my number one recommendation for anyone wanting to understand the Craft. Although not specifically woman-oriented, this book is written in an easy-to-understand style and starts from the very beginning with no assumptions about the reader's knowledge of the Craft. It provides the basics of magic, Craft concepts of time and space, how to identify negative Craft, a history of Witchcraft, and an explanation of karma and reincarnation, all in the first half of the book. The second half is centered on personal applications of magic. It includes beginning information on astrology and tarot, but I feel the most important, by far, is the chapter is on Words of Power. Weinstein explains how to create and use Words of Power. In essence, Words of Power are spells, but Weinstein takes away the mystery and details how to bring the Craft into one's daily life. This is the kind of book you can give to your family and friends if you want them to understand your interest in Witchcraft. I've recommended it to hundreds of women and, so far, no one has expressed disappointment.

*Drawing Down the Moon** by Margot Adler

This book has been a classic in the mainstream Pagan movement since its publication in 1979. It reminds me of a sociological study of the Craft. The chapter on feminism and the Craft provides an accurate assessment of the women's spiritual community. The information included in this book outlines the basic beliefs and philosophy of Witches, Druids, Goddess-worshippers, and other Pagans. Adler explores the traditions that exist and outlines the differences and similarities in their beliefs and practices. Revised in 1987, it now includes information about Fairie (gay) men and updated information on many of the subjects included in the original work. The comprehensive resource listings in the revised edition provide access to many of the groups and publications which are well known in the Craft today.

*The Spiral Dance** by Starhawk

The Spiral Dance is thought to have started thousands of covens. It is well written with a style which is often more like poetry than prose. It is a combination of basic Craft philosophy with information detailing how to do various rituals and exercises. In *The Spiral Dance*, Starhawk says that the underlying philosophy is from the Faery tradition which is, if one may judge by her book, a tradition which includes a concept of male divinity. This concept of a male deity is not shared by all women practicing women's spirituality and, for them, the chapter on the god may not be of interest. Starhawk's overall orientation is feminist, however, and the *The Spiral Dance* is a classic found in the library of almost every Witch.

*Mother Wit** by Diane Mariechild

Mother Wit is a book about psychic development. It consists mainly of explanations and exercises which identify, encourage, and use psychic skills. It includes basic work on relaxation and clearing and then moves along to energy work, psychic communication, and an excellent chapter on healing. *Mother Wit* is one of the few books which includes information about psychic work with children. As the book progresses, it moves into discussions and exercises about reincarnation, dreams, and Witchcraft. Following the exercises in this book can lead to a heightened sense of psychic awareness and an understanding of how to bring one's psychic skills into use.

*The Politics of Women's Spirituality** edited by Charlene Spretnak

This is a massive compilation of essays by many different women including Merlin Stone, Adrienne Rich, Starhawk, Gloria Steinem, Mary Daly, Z. Budapest. Those who are extremely well read in feminist Craft may find some duplication, but for those who are new to the Craft, it is a vast resource of thealogy, philosophy, and practice as it relates to the spiritual women's community. This book is very much based on women's spiritual experience and on the rise of feminist spirituality within the women's movement.

Fiction

*The Mists of Avalon** by Marion Zimmer Bradley

For some women, sitting down to plow their way through a seemingly vast scholastic text in order to gain some basic information about the matriarchy is either no fun or not a way which they choose to gain a working knowledge of the Craft. If you are one of these women or if you just like to read stories which help to keep wonder alive, *The Mists of Avalon* may be just the answer. Marion Zimmer Bradley is well known as a prolific science fiction/fantasy writer. She is known also in Pagan circles for having published a letter in the *Covenant of the Goddess Newsletter* stating that she takes the Craft very seriously. Many people believe *The Mists of Avalon* to be her best work to date. It tells the Arthurian legend from the perspective of English Pagans being greeted by the early Christian religion and dogma. This book is extremely insightful and descriptive of the attitudes of both the Pagan folk toward the Christians and those of the Christians toward the Pagans. It is also a well-told tale.

Daughters of Copper Woman* by Anne Cameron

This is a delightful book which blends the stories and legends of the Native American Nootka people with the stories of the women of Vancouver Island, British Columbia, today in such a way that it is difficult to identify where the stories stop and a quiet truth begins. These tales, like *The Mists of Avalon*, deal with the arrival of Christians to the island. The simple strength of the women who attempt to preserve their culture and heritage while under assault from the "long robes" is inspiring. The stories in this book blend together in such a way that the Nookta's underlying matriarchal values are shown as a natural part of these Native people.

Matriarchy

When God Was a Woman* by Merlin Stone

This book is not light reading. *When God Was a Woman* is a detailed, scholastic account of the demise of matriarchy in the fertile crescent. Stone goes point by point, using many sources, including the Bible, to document how matriarchal culture was, over a period of several hundred years, successfully destroyed in this area of the world. Additionally, she traces the status of women in these countries and leaves no doubt that the rights and opportunities of women in matriarchal culture far exceded those that women have experienced since.

The First Sex* by Elizabeth Gould Davis

This book was one of the earliest attempts to document and explain matriarchy. It was the first book I read that helped me to understand the connection between traditional religion and women's oppression. Although criticized by some scholars for lack of documentation, the book makes a convincing case for the phenomenon of global matriarchy and its gradual decline as a result of governmental and religious doctrine which sought to strip women of their power. For Davis, this book seems to have been a work of passion, and her strong feelings about women's strength shine through on every page.

The Woman's Encyclopedia of Myths and Secrets* by Barbara Walker

This is a monumental work with 1,120 pages of information organized in an easy-to-access encyclopedia form. It is a wonderful reference and resource book containing entries useful for everything from serious study to entertainment. Walker has compiled an astounding mass of information that ranges from Goddess trivia to the profoundly insightful. She has traced the etymology of words that are commonly used to define women and Goddess culture back to their original woman-centered meanings. *The Woman's Encyclopedia of Myths and Secrets* shares information about the origins of words and other hidden information, the beginnings of which have been forgotten. I keep my copy where I can read an entry every time I have a few extra moments.

■ Hints about Finding and Evaluating Spiritual Books

Any time one begins to search the shelves of bookstores for books and information about women's spirituality or the Craft, intuition plays a key role. Many of the books which are published as books about Witchcraft include information designed to be sensational and/or include negative or manipulative practices. Some of these books are easy to spot because they proclaim that they can show you the secrets of the universe for only $12.95. Books which allegedly show how to get the one you love, to have the riches you deserve, or to get rid of your boss are most likely encouraging negative Craft practices. Books which promote manipulation, ask you to defame another religion, or include hexes, curses or binding spells are definitely treading on dangerous ground in terms of manipulative magic.

There is a second category of books, which are more subtle, that one might want to be on the watch for. These are books which pose as positive Craft publications but which contain some negative elements. Many of these books contain information that might be considered negative or manipulative, but they also contain some of the most basic, undiluted explanations of the Craft as it is and has been practiced. I find the latter extremely refreshing. However, many of these books contend that negative and/or manipulative magic is a tradition reflecting a certain heritage or ethnic origin merely because someone's mother, grandmother, or great-grandmother included such activities. This contention, along with its companion position that this "tradition" should be preserved, is, I feel, most often invalid. If you decide to read about the Craft (including what you're reading now), remember to evaluate the information presented from the standpoint of positive practice and how it strikes you personally on a gut level. Remember, too, that in the Craft, you are the one, true judge of your own spiritual practice.

When looking for books about the Craft, there is a series of logical places to start. If you have a women's bookstore in your area, start there. Most women's bookstores have a section of spiritual books in which you will probably be able to find many of the titles mentioned above. In areas where there is no women's bookstore, there are two other likely places to look next—an occult bookstore or a New Age bookstore. Either one of these may carry some woman-centered publications. They often have a women's section that will likely contain some books about women's spirituality. If you don't see what you want, most bookstores (even regular, mainstream stores) will order a book for you. A word of caution: some occult bookstores cater to an audience which participates in negative magic practices. Trust your intuition. If you feel uncomfortable with either the patrons or the staff in a store, either don't go in or don't go back.

In some areas none of these options exist. If you can't find any of these types of stores or if you feel uncomfortable buying books about the Craft in your hometown, then mail order may be your best option. *The Gaia Catalog** is an excellent resource for women's spiritual books and other related products. Many women's bookstores offer mail order services. In addition, some of the Pagan papers offer many of these books by mail order and some of these titles are available directly from their publishers.

■ *The Performing Arts*

Many things can be considered performing arts, but, in general, music and drama seem to be thought of as the primary expressions of this art form. Within the women's spiritual and Pagan cultures, drama is an area which has yet to be greatly explored. There are occasional, isolated performances with a Goddess orientation, but these are rare. One notable exception is Z. Budapest's play *The Rise of the Fates** which has been performed several times since it was published in 1976. Unlike drama, however, women's spiritual and Pagan music have already become strong elements of these new cultures.

Music has long been thought to have a spiritual power, and this power has not gone unrecognized by women of spirit. In the reemergence of women's spirituality, music has increasingly played a part in both ceremony and celebration. Music which affirms women's spiritual feelings is often represented among women's music performers, and spiritually oriented music now comes in almost all musical styles including rock, jazz, classical, modern, folk, and traditional music. One style of music which is particularly popular among women of spirit is chants. Chanting is the most used musical form in ritual. Music in general and chants in particular are considered an excellent way to form a group bond and to raise energy for ritual.

In the earliest days of the feminist movement, women realized that the life experiences and feelings of women are not often reflected in traditional musical options of mainstream culture (such as rock and top 40). At best, this music tends to depict women as powerless and to speak of them only in relation to men (with a few notable exceptions by some women performers). At worst, this music glorifies violence toward women and encourages the degradation of women. Women became interested in having music which was affirming of their experience and which was written from a woman-centered perspective. During the seventies, many musical forms emerged which sought to fill this need. This music is most often simply called "women's music," and it has enjoyed a growing popularity since the mid-seventies. Women's music reflects the diverse feelings and life experiences of lesbians and of feminists. It is music which affirms their loves, their political work, and, increasingly, their spirituality. This is the music which one will find being played at "women's music festivals" like the Michigan Womyn's Music Festival and the New England Women's Music Retreat (see Chapter Four for other information about festivals). Many women's music performers now have some spiritual content in their music, while some of these performers do primarily spiritual music.

Among the better known of women's music performers with a reputation for performing spiritual music is Kay Gardner.* Gardner has been working within the women's music industry since its beginnings. She has a background in classical music, and her work reflects this training. She has recorded six albums to date, "Mooncircles," "Emerging," "A Rainbow Path," "Fishersdaughter," "Avalon" and "Garden of Ecstasy." Most of the music on these albums is instrumental with only occasional vocals, and many of the selections reflect a stong Goddess orientation. "A Rainbow Path" is a particularly interesting album. The recordings on it are specifically made to resonate with tones, colors, and the different chakra points. The information accompanying the album explains the research which Gardner has done in connecting these melodies to the chakras and her exploration of modes of music which she considers to be particularly woman-oriented.

Two other women's performers who have a strong spiritual orientation in their music are Ruth Barrett and Cyntia Smith.* Their music is Celtic in style and performed with dulcimer accompaniment. Many of the pieces on their albums "Aeolus," "Rolling World," and "Deepening" celebrate the Goddess and the cyclic, seasonal patterns of the Celtic calendar. Their music includes haunting vocals and unusual dulcimer accompaniment. "Every Woman Born" is a song performed on their "Aeolus" album. It is a very moving piece which tells of the connection of the Goddess to the Take Back the Night movement. It was written by Barrett for Z. Budapest's fortieth birthday.

Many women's music performers have spiritual content in some of their songs. Rhiannon,* Willie Tyson,* Alix Dobkin,* Linda Shear, Debbie Fier,* and many others have songs which acknowledge womanspirit. Perhaps not as well known but with music that strongly focuses on women of spirit are Libana,* Cindee Grace,* Susan Arrow and the Quivers,* Catherine Madsen,* and Karen Mackay.*

Recordings by most of these artists are available at women's bookstores and at women's festivals and gatherings. If these are not accessible to you, most of the recordings are also available through the mail from the Ladyslipper Catalog.* The numbers of spiritual women's music performers are growing; music which celebrates a woman-centered spirituality and culture is increasingly available. The future is sure to bring more performers and more music which celebrates the Goddess in each woman.

As in other areas, alongside the women's movement, the Pagan movement has also developed its own music. As differentiated from women's music, the music of Pagans is more often strictly spiritual. There is less blending of other life experiences and spirituality. If one is looking for music which speaks primarily about spirituality, Pagan music has this advantage over most women's music. However, many of the cautions previously mentioned about publications carry into Pagan music; in other words, the role of women in this music varies widely. Music which celebrates the Horned God and/or the duality of the Goddess and God is common. The best supplier of Pagan music is Circle.* Their catalog lists music by Jim Alan, Gwydion Pendderwen, Kenny and Tzipora Klein, Angie Remedi, and others.

■ Visual Arts

Nowhere has the Goddess movement had a more profound effect than on the art and imagery of the women's movement. The symbols of the

Goddess are everywhere among the art, crafts, and other creative work of the women's community. Increasingly over the past few years, the items offered for sale by craftswomen at festivals and in women's bookstores include a spiritual orientation. One can now find jewelry with a wide range of symbols from Goddess religion and even tiny statues of actual Goddesses. The Goddess and her symbols are now appearing in glass, in wood, in fiber, in stone, and even on bumper stickers. These symbols provide images and ideas which help form and enhance the concepts of women's spirituality.

In addition to the surge of spiritual-oriented crafts and benchwork, there has also been an increase in spiritual graphics and art. One of the main places for women to display their artwork is on the covers and in the pages of the women's spiritual publications. Art which celebrates and affirms the Goddess and women's spirituality greets one in many of these publications. As mentioned in Chapter Five, there are now several women's tarot decks with images developed by women. These decks give whole systems of symbols linked to the relationship between art and revelatory experience.

One of the premier artists of the women's spiritual movement is Sudie Rakusin. Rakusin's work is alive with portraits of Goddesses who seem to be both ancient archetypes and contemporary. Her art graces many of the covers of women's spiritual publications. Her journals,* *Dreams and Shadows* and *Goddesses and Amazons* include many images of Goddesses and Goddess women. Rakusin's art does not stand alone; other fine artists like Prairie Jackson, Joann Colbert and Max Dashu are also working to celebrate and reclaim the Goddess in picture and icon. The muses thought to inspire the creative process have come alive among today's women of spirit. Increasingly, art which reflects a Goddess orientation is being created and celebrated.

■ Education

Many women are anxious to learn about feminist religion, and much of the activity in the women's spiritual community today involves developing ways to share this knowledge. The women's community has long held a different attitude toward education from that of society at large. Traditional education is considered proscriptive, with someone who is supposedly knowledgeable on a particular topic telling you what you must know in order to consider yourself informed on that topic. They define for you the order in which you must learn this information and then dangle recognition and credentials as a reward. This competitive hierarchical attitude toward gaining knowledge is not seen as compatible with the philosophy of the women's movement in general and women's spirituality in particular.

This means that those interested in passing along information about women's spirituality to others are redefining both the philosophy and the methods of education. This redefinition has led many women to view education as a non-directive, non-competitive, and non-hierarchical process. There are no classes or workshops that one can take and emerge Wise; rather, piece by piece from many different sources, knowledge is gained. "Teachers" do not design this process for "students." Each woman's progress toward wisdom is individual. "Teachers" can and do share their knowledge and experiences in hopes that these will be helpful to others, but most often, they do not consider their own education to be complete. This form of education is more like sharing than teaching. Although the "teacher" may have much to give to the "students," it is seldom that the "students" have nothing to give in return. Spiritual women are attempting to take education out of its traditional, hierarchical form and to share their knowledge in a supportive process which empowers the students and which is more compatible with women's growth and learning styles.

These new ways of sharing knowledge are taking form, and information about women's spirituality is being passed on through workshops, retreats, talks, intensives, local community discussions, and ritual groups. Many of the writers, artists and musicians in women's spirituality do public speaking and give workshops. The festivals and gatherings of the women's community are filled with workshops and discussions that range from "how-to" information to in-depth studies of women's spiritual practices. Increasingly, there are gatherings which are solely spiritual in nature. These can be weekend intensives or longer programs like the Witchcamp held in Canada.

Probably the most effective teaching tool, however, is the closed ritual or discussion group. It is at these intimate gatherings that women are learning about themselves and the Craft in a personal way that can be most easily incorporated into their daily lives. For most women in the Craft, there is no outside expert. It is the information that they find within themselves that is used to guide them on their spiritual journeys. At times, many women seem to long for some great leader, guru, or sage to come along and reveal to them the "secrets." This, however, is the antithesis of Craft teachings which glorify the Goddess within.

Women's Craft does not lend itself to producing directive leadership and education. I frequently advise women not to spend time searching for a female Obi-Wan Kenobi, but to spend that time seeking within themselves for the answers that they hope such a teacher would provide.

With women of spirit there are, occasionally, exceptions to this philosophy. One may find a woman setting herself up as a master teacher, great leader, or even as a dictatorial high priestess. There are even women who are willing to and interested in "following" these self-styled leaders. It has been my experience, however, that this style of spiritual instruction does not last long in the women's spiritual community. Women have become aware of what happens when they give away their power and are, for the most part, not interested in continuing that experience within a spiritual context.

■ *Wellness, Women, and Witches: A Philosophy of Healing*

Wellness among spiritual women is strongly considered a part of education. Throughout time, spirituality and healing have been closely intertwined. Spirit-healing is probably the oldest form of healing known. It is not surprising that cultures which remained close to their matriarchal origins maintained the idea that it was difficult, if not impossible, to heal the body without healing the mind and spirit. Cultures late to encounter modern medicine still hold a matriarchal attitude toward healing, which includes an emphasis on wellness and the holistic treatment of dis-ease. Within these cultures, a priestess, shaman, or Witch doctor was (and, in some cases, still is) seen as both a spiritual leader and as a healing practitioner. Spirit-healers of old typically used a holistic approach to medicine which included magic and religion within a healing context. This concept acknowledged not only the healing of the physical body but also the roles of the mental and emotional state of the individual seeking assistance. Healing was not a specialization practiced in isolation from the other activities of the community as we see it practiced in mainstream medicine today. It was, instead, based on the whole person, including her relationships to herself, to her community, and to her spiritual condition. The spirit-healer addressed the total person and was seen as a catalyst for healing the physical, emotional, and social ills of her friends and family.

Changes came as patriarchal thought began to influence the practice of healing. Healing of the total individual was gradually replaced by medicine as a science with its isolated, specialized approach. Doctors, often not connected to patients in any other way, diagnose for one system or organ alone, many times without information or regard for the forms or circumstances of the person's life. The emphasis is on the elimination of symptoms, and it often includes invasive techniques that violate the individual physically and psychically.

When patriarchal cultures began their domination, information on healing that was deemed useful was gathered from the spirit-healers and incorporated into Western medical practice. The use of digitalis for heart ailments is an example of this. Digitalis was well known to British lay healers, who shared information about this curative herb with members of the emerging male medical community. This sharing was not of benefit to the spirit-healers. The new medical practitioners lobbied and legislated what would be "real" medicine, eliminating and/or making it illegal to practice alternatives. The spirit-healer's role in the community diminished and finally disappeared.

The healing philosophy of feminist Witchcraft carries forth and re-creates the concepts of healing practiced by the spirit-healers of the matriarchy. The healing techniques currently being practiced and developed by feminist Witches include the concepts of wholeness and the holistic treatment of illness. They stress a balanced integration of body, mind, and spirit, and not just an absence of disease. Right living, which sets a balance and which honors the relationship between the body, mind, and spirit, is considered the road to maintaining wellness. The maximum health/wellness of the individual is the ultimate aim of all healing activities.

In keeping with the basic philosophy of Wicca, the philosophy of healing holds that there is a unified system of cause and effect that produces all form and substance. This system of cause and effect sets in motion certain energy patterns that manifest in women's lives as health or illness. Healing is based on this principle. The conscious and the unconscious direction(s) of this energy through and within our bodies is what creates health or illness. If energy flowing through our bodies is balanced and unimpeded, then we are healthy. If, however, there are physical, mental, or emotional blocks in our systems and the energy in our bodies is restricted or confined, then illness may result.

Healers within women's Wicca are viewed as catalysts. They do not take personal credit or responsibility for any healing that may take place. They solicit information from the persons seeking wholeness and offer the individuals new ways of assessing their situation.

Healers incorporate their intuitive understanding of the situation with their own energy and with that of the seeker into a healing process. They are a channel for a universal energy force. The role of the healer is to reconnect the individual with her own spiritual forces, to restore balance, and to promote the wellness of the individual according to her own ability to heal and become whole. Healing is not something that is done to someone; it is done with them. Within the women's community, this concept is so valued that there has even been discussion that the use of the term "healer" inaccurately describes these catalysts, and some feminist Witches are in search of a word that will convey this role of helping individuals seeking to become whole. Weller, catalyzer, or transformer have all been suggested as words that explain more accurately what should be happening in the interaction between the individuals seeking wholeness and their guide or assistant in this process.

Among Wiccan women healers, there is also a belief in the mind as an equal partner in the healing process. The effectiveness of the medicine women or shamans may have only been partially based on their technical healing knowledge and skill. Medical science has often shown the effects of placebo medication on an individual. Persons given substances which should have no effect their condition report relief from their symptoms when told the medication administered will have a positive effect. If the individuals are told the medication will have side effects, two thirds of them report experiencing these side effects. As further evidence of this phenomenon, if the person administering the medication believes the medication will be effective on the condition, then the relief experienced by the individual taking the medication increases dramatically. Having stubbornly clung to the concept that the mind plays a major role in any illness, women healers attempt to enlist the participation of the individual's rational functions in the healing process. Changing the mental assumptions and expectations of individuals can be a key factor in their return to total health and wellness.

In addition to the roles of the mind and the body in healing, Wiccan healing practitioners also acknowledge the relationship of the spiritual state of the individuals seeking to become whole with their physical condition. To help heal a body or mind and leave a soul unattended is only doing part of the healer's work. Women's healing is often coupled with ritual. Ritual speaks to the "deep mind"—the spirit within—in the language of symbols. Ritual, words of power, chanting, and spell work communicate the possibility of change to our spirit-selves.

Within our spirit-selves lies the source of true healing; a woman who can act as a catalyst to awaken this part of our healing energy is truly a spirit-healer.

The Wiccan Concept of Illness

Illness is not viewed as the whim of capricious fate. Many feminist Witches believe that illness is meant to tell you something. Pain and disease are viewed as information, as signals from our bodies to us. To mask or eliminate pain without analyzing the cause may simply risk that similar symptoms will appear in some other place or system of our bodies. Pain and disease are not necessarily negative but may be our bodies' attempts to communicate to us that certain areas of our lives need attention. Illness is viewed as an opportunity for individual growth. The process of assessing what in our body, mind, or spirit has caused or is causing dis-ease to manifest itself is a major form of diagnosis in healing by women Witches. Achieving one's maximum potential for health and wellness through listening to oneself and seeking information about what is out of balance is the desired result of all healing work.

As mentioned in Chapter Two, if our attitudes, beliefs, and words create the forms and circumstances of our lives, then they can also create disease or wellness. People who think that they are basically unhealthy increase the likelihood that they will manifest ill-health in their lives. If, however, these persons restructure their thinking to view themselves as totally healthy individuals, then the chances of attaining optimal wellness increase. Our words can also shape our reality. A person who continually tells herself that she needs a break from work may find herself with a broken leg. Viewing something or someone as a pain in the neck may mainfest. More frightening statements in this catagory include: "if _____ happens, I will just die," and "_____ scares me to death."

Closely linked to manifesting our reality from our words is the concept of illness as a metaphor for life circumstances. Examples of possible equations of diseases to life circumstances are given by Diane Mariechild in *Mother Wit*:

"Arm and Hand Problems: inability to get a grasp on things; problems with manipulation; inability to express yourself creatively.

"Asthma or Breathing Problems: person, attitude, or situation that is suffocating you; something that you can't get off your chest.

"Shoulder Problems: feeling like you carry the weight of the world on your shoulders; saviour complex."[6]

As these examples demonstrate, finding the site of a dis-ease can give information and assistance in determining a course of action that can be taken toward a holistic approach to treatment.

In the Western concept of medicine, disease is viewed as a thing to be conquered. We hear of the stamping out of smallpox and the hope for extermination of cancer and AIDS within our lifetimes. The patriarchal attitude apparent in other areas of thought carries forth into medical thought. The idea of conquering nature, presented in Genesis, seems to spill over into patriarchal attitudes toward dealing with disease. Wars are waged against cancer; patients battle with arthritis; and we add drugs to our arsenal. This idea of illness as something foreign to be battled with and brought under control is not one that is generally accepted in Wiccan healing thought.

Instead, disease and healing are also thought of as processes. We, our bodies, minds, and spirts, are not closed systems, but constantly changing ones. Our bodies replace themselves regularly over varying periods of time for different systems and structures. For example, we replace the cells in our skeletal structures every seven years. If disease is viewed as a process, then the dysfunctions which we find in our physical, mental, or spiritual systems today need not continue to be incorporated into these systems which we are constantly creating anew. The patriarchal medical approach tends to interrupt the process with intervention which masks the symptoms and/or removes the site of the manifestation. In so doing, Western medicine may cause the person to remain out of balance and to remove the information that is needed to understand what is necessary to begin becoming whole.

This is another area where Wiccan healers are suggesting linguistic change along with systematic and philosophical shifts. The way that we have been taught to speak of disease promotes a Western medical view. Small linguistic changes could assist in viewing disease as a process. Referring to a disease with a noun encourages thinking of disease as a thing. If, however, we consider changing the noun to a verb, it conveys a very different attitude. An example of such a change is "fluing" instead of "having the flu." These subtle changes encourage us to accept the process and our responsibility for it. In some cases, this action alone can bring incredible change in the condition of the person who is seeking wholeness. Denial of what is happening, fear of what will happen, or resentment about the form and circumstances of an illness can be primary causes in the perpetuation of those circumstances. This knowledge was an intuitive part the spirit-healers' "cure," and today women Witches are seeking to incorporate these attitudes again into their healing philosophy.

Stress

No discussion of holistic healing would be complete without discussing the role of stress. Stress, technically speaking, is the body's response to change. In our fast-paced culture, it may seem to our bodies, minds, or spirits that things are continually changing. Rapid transportation can change our location by thousands of miles in a few hours; rapid communication brings us an influx of news and information we may be unprepared to deal with; the transitory nature of our society may disturb our relationships with family and friends; technology outpaces our ability to comprehend its impact and use; and metropolitan culture removes us from nature and our natural cycles. With stimulation of a modern culture so much more intense than that experienced by our ancestors, it is a testimony to the flexibility of our spirits, minds, and bodies that we have been able to adapt to it in such a short period of time.

The pressures of modern society have caused a plague of modern stress-related diseases. Stress-related diseases range from the mildly uncomfortable to the deadly. High blood pressure, colitis, heart disease, headaches, and stroke are only some of the diseases with known links to stress. What does stress have to do with women's healing and spirituality? One goal of women's healing is to have an expanded sense of self. In order to remain expanded, one must be able to adjust to change. As pointed out earlier, stress is a response to change. Stress is a signal from our bodies, minds, or spirits that we need to consider making change. Stress, in and of itself, is not positive or negative. Learning to listen to these stress messages, and to adapt to change in our lives with as much ease and grace as possible, is a positive use of stress.

In keeping with the concept of balance, feminist Witches are advocating balance within medical systems. Not all the "advances" in medical science are necessarily negative. Many of the diagnostic techniques and some surgical procedures can be used effectively if these techniques are balanced with attention to the forms and circumstances of a person's life. Most often, women Wiccans are open to accepting ideas which do not conflict with the basic beliefs of Wicca, and healing techniques are no exception to this rule. Women healers are integrating both Western and non-Western medical approaches. Recent surveys indicate that the Western medical community is beginning to feel the pressure of the consumer who is now looking for holistic care.

It has long been a concept in the Craft that if you do not find what you seek within yourself, you will not find it elsewhere. If you wish for peace, be and act in peaceful ways; if you wish for a world of love, act lovingly toward all with whom you come in contact; if you desire to encounter truth, speak the truth yourself. If we wish to heal the Earth of the injuries that mankind has wrought, we must first heal ourselves. With every woman who becomes whole, we gain another link in the chain which will lead to the healing of the planet. The personal is political. We are a macrocosm of the universe, and in healing ourselves, we heal both each other and our planet.

■ Pagan Children

Since the beginning of time, through both the matriarchal and patriarchal eras, women have been primarily responsible for teaching children about the culture in which they live. Women today are no exception; within the women's spiritual community there is a growing interest in passing along Craft philosophy and tradition to younger generations. However, making the decision to include children in a nontraditional religion is not without its hazards. Children who participate in celebrations and activities can pass on information to ex-husbands, teachers, and grandparents who may be less than enthusiastic about having a child taught Witchcraft. In a few cases, this has even instigated custody battles from frightened parents or partners. Including a child in Pagan activities means either the parent must be willing to educate individuals her child might choose to confide in, or the child must learn at an early age the value of keeping the silence.

A major reason why some feminist Witches have become involved in mainstream Paganism is because they are mothers of boy children. Many mothers feel that it is important for young boys to know other Pagan men and to see other men celebrating the Goddess. Within women's spirituality, very few options are available for young males. Most women's groups, in fact, formally do little with children regardless of their gender. It appears that mothers are not prepared to deal with the ramifications of incorporating children into rituals or other Pagan activities. This does not mean, however, that children are not educated about the Goddess and the Craft, but it seems this takes place primarily in the home rather than in public. In keeping with feminist Wiccan thealogy, mothers want to be sure that children are making their own choices about their spiritual beliefs and are not pressured by others.

Mainstream Paganism, however, features many activities for children, and children are often part of the focus for seasonal celebrations. Because mainstream Paganism is more likely to include traditional family groupings, children are more often present at Pagan events. There are even Pagan Parents' Leagues,* organizations dedicated to helping Pagan parents to integrate their spirituality into the daily lives of their children and to teach their children the values implied by a nature religion. Aside from being a slight embarrassment to some teenagers, most children of Pagans seem to accept, appreciate, and enjoy sharing in the spiritual activities of their families.

There is an increasing number of Pagan-oriented children's books. A particularly good publication called *Pagan Kids* is available from New Leaf Distribution.* This book is filled with information about the Craft and activities which children can do that bring the Craft to life. Another book available from New Leaf is a *Coloring Book of Goddesses*; it is difficult to decide whether this is a book for children or for the child in each of us.

The passing of the Craft from parent to child is traditionally how Wicca has been taught and kept alive for generations. "Fam trads" or Family Tradition Witches who were taught the Craft by their parents or other family members many times boast of a long line of Wiccan ancestors. Although not common in either the women's spiritual or Pagan communities, these "fam trads" as the children of spiritual women and neo-Pagans grow into Witches in their own right.

■ Reactions to Pagan Culture

Whether in regard to children or adults, how much to tell others about one's participation in the Craft is an important decision for many women. "Coming out of the broom closet" can have dramatic consequences. There have been both public and private persecutions of women whose association with the Craft has become public. Women have been fired from their jobs, had their leases terminated, have been sued for custody of their children, and have been subjected to other even more difficult actions when their affiliation with the Craft has become known. Unfortunately, the popular definition of Witchcraft in mainstream culture is closely linked to Satanism. Many people believe that Witches are negative or manipulative and that they have made pacts with evil spirits. This means any time a woman decides to share her identity as a Witch with others, she assumes some risk. How much risk depends largely on whom she decides to tell and the environment in which she lives.

It was not until 1950 that the laws against Witchcraft were repealed in England, and in many areas of the United States there are still laws against charging for divinatory readings. These laws seem, in part, designed to suppress this mainstay of the Craft community. Because of centuries of negative association, there are still attitudes ranging from subtle prejudice to outright hatred of anything associated with Witchcraft. Many Christians, especially fundamentalists, tend to have a most unfavorable response to the Craft. Because fundamentalists believe in a literal interpretation of the Bible, statements such as "Thou shalt not suffer a Witch to live"[7] may be applied precisely.

I would like to point out that I have lived since 1975 as an "out" Witch. Virtually all of the people with whom I have been in contact have known of my identification with Witchcraft. I have spoken at events, have been on radio and television, have worked with an international network, and have never suffered any negative consequences. I do not feel there is any need to keep your association with the Craft totally secret, but at the same time, a little discretion can go a long way toward warding off potential problems.

With the growth of women's and Pagan spirituality there has been a general backlash from the right wing. Unfortunately, some of the people who are most uninformed and/or reactionary about the Craft are in positions of power. Periodically officials try to adopt legislation which will deny the Craft the status of a religion. A national example of this was an amendment to a postal bill proposed in September of 1985 by Senator Jesse Helms of North Carolina. This postal bill was targeted because several women's spiritual and Pagan organizations have been recognized as non-profit religious organizations and, therefore, can receive reduced bulk mailing rates. The legislation proposed that, "No funds appropriated under this act shall be used to grant, maintain, or allow tax exemption to any cult, organization, or other group that has as a purpose or that has any interest in the promoting of Satanism or Witchcraft; provided that for purposes of this section, 'Satanism' is defined as the worship of Satan or the powers of evil, and 'Witchcraft' is defined as the use of powers derived from evil spirits, the use of sorcery, or the use of supernatural powers with malicious intent."[8]

Although most Wiccans felt that this legislation did not, in fact, apply to them because of their dedication to a positive path, it was thought this legislation was aimed at Wiccan groups because of a letter read into the Congressional Record by Helms. The letter stated, "Under [IRS] standards, several organizations have been recognized as tax-exempt that espouse a system of beliefs, rituals, and practices, derived in part from pre-Christian Celtic and Welsh traditions, which they label as "WitchCraft."' While he did present the letter for inclusion in the Congressional Record, he did not quote the rest of the letter which said that the IRS already had sufficient safeguards to prevent dangerous and unlawful groups from having exempt status and the IRS found no evidence that any of the Craft groups granted exempt status were engaged in any illegal activity. Instead, Helms erroneously claimed the contrary, saying: "We allow tax exempt status for bona fide religious organizations because we believe they help promote the common good. . .Witchcraft groups do not—in fact they lead to violent and unlawful behavior."[9]

The response to this bill by women's spiritual and Pagan groups was strong. Aided by the American Civil Liberties Union, women and Pagans from across the country called, wrote, and organized in opposition to this proposed legislation and circles were organized to preserve religious freedom. When a Joint Congressional committee met on October 31, 1985 (Halloween) to consider the amendment, there was no one who would speak out in its favor. Amendment 705 was stopped at the Joint Committee level.

This is only one example of the backlash caused by the recognition of these emerging cultures by the larger society. A bill similar to the Helms amendment was introduced by Senator Robert Walker to Congress in 1985 and met a similar fate. Additionally, there continue to be increasing reports of isolated harrassment, job action, and custody issues associated with Craft religious practitioners. The Helms amendment, however, caused the women's and Pagan communities to organize and prepare for similar events. The Covenant of the Goddess (see Chapter Four) reawakened its efforts toward public awareness, and Circle Network began the Pagan Strength Web, a "network within Circle Network formed to protect religious freedom for Wiccans and other Pagans and to give spiritual support to those harrassed because of their religion."[10] Increasingly, there are actions to have Wiccan holidays recognized as legitimate religious holidays, attempts to provide protection for Wiccans in employment, and efforts to allow Craft practitioners who are incarcerated to celebrate and practice their chosen religion.

■ Resources

Recommended Readings

Marion Weinstein, *Positive Magic: Occult Self-Help*. Custer, Washington: Phoenix Publishing Co., 1981.

Margot Adler, *Drawing Down the Moon*. Boston: Beacon Press, 1986.

Starhawk, *The Spiral Dance*. San Francisco: Harper & Row, 1979.

Diane Mariechild, *Mother Wit*. Trumansburg, New York: The Crossing Press, 1981.

Charlene Spretnak, ed., *The Politics of Women's Spirituality*. Garden City, New York: Anchor Press/Doubleday, 1982.

Marion Zimmer Bradley, *The Mists of Avalon*. New York: Alfred A. Knopf, 1983.

Anne Cameron, *Daughters of Copper Woman*. Vancouver, B.C.: Press Gang Publishers, 1985.

Merlin Stone, *When God Was a Woman*. New York: The Dial Press, 1976.

Elizabeth Gould Davis, *The First Sex*. Baltimore: Penguin Books, Inc., 1971.

Barbara Walker, *The Woman's Encyclopedia of Myths and Secrets*. San Francisco: Harper & Row, 1983.

■ Periodicals and Papers

The information in the following listings was provided by the publishers.

Women's Papers and Periodicals

Arachne is about the search for and practice of women's spirituality, focusing on female aspects of divinity; respect for the Goddess, past and present, is very much linked to respect for women. Contributions of original research, rituals, line drawings, poems, and more along these lines are welcome. Write for sample; semi-annual; 4.50 pounds sterling plus 1.20 pounds for airmail to US; 3.50 pounds in Europe: *Arachne*, c/o 14 Hill Crest, Sevenoaks, Kent, England.

The Gaia Catalog (formerly *WomanSpirit Catalogue*) is a source for womanspirit resources and artistic creations; listings include audio tapes, bookstores, clothing and jewelry, music, tarot, and unique gifts: *The Gaia Catalog*, 1400 Shattuck Ave. # 9, Berkeley, CA 94709.

Goddess Rising is a journal of wimmin's spirituality published by Goddess Rising Dianic Wicce Shop; $1.50 for sample; quarterly; $6.00 US; $8.00 outside US (US funds only): Goddess Rising, 4006 First NE, Seattle, WA 98105.

Octava is a four-page newsletter largely composed of letters from readers. $1.25 for sample; 8 times a year; $10.00: Octava, P.O. Box 8, Clear Lake, WA 98235.

Of a Like Mind is a newspaper for spiritual ♀. Articles on dreams, tarot, astrology, wellness, herbs, psychic development, craft, Goddesses, herstory, and more from a womon-centered perspective; open forum for more informal sharing; extensive networking section; announcements; events; graphics; reviews. $3.00 for sample; quarterly; $13/21/33 (sliding scale); add $5.00 for first class or outside USA: OALM, P.O. Box 6021, Madison, WI 53716.

SageWoman Magazine is a journal of women's spirituality celebrating the Goddess in each woman. Similar to *WomanSpirit Magazine*; 40–50 pages of magic, wisdom, and inspiration. $4.50 for sample; quarterly; $13 US; $15 international: *SageWoman Magazine*, P.O. Box 5130, Santa Cruz, CA 95063.

Thesmophoria is focused on Feminist Wicca as the New Women's religion. Articles, letters, reviews, a local events calendar, ads, poetry, and graphics. Write for sample; 8 times a year; $7-$10 (sliding scale); $13.25 outside the USA; US funds only: *Thesmophoria*, Susan B. Anthony Coven #1, P.O. Box 11363, Oakland, CA 94611.

Woman of Power, a magazine of feminism, spirituality, and politics. Each issue revolves around a specific theme such as Nature, Making Peace, Science and Technology, Woman's Experience and the Sacred, and Money and Work. Write for sample; bi-annual; $22 US; $26 Canada and other countries: *Woman of Power*, P.O. Box 827, Cambridge, MA 02238.

WomanSpirit is no longer publishing, but it is still a fascinating, timeless treasury of a decade of women's spiritual sharing. Back issues are each 64 pp. of beauty, challenge, and inspiration; $ 3.00 each. Send addressed, stamped envelope for list: *WomanSpirit*, 2000 King Mountain Trail, Wolf Creek, OR 97497.

Mainstream Pagan Papers and Periodicals

The Bard is a journal dedicated to their family religion, rooted in Welsh-Celtic, pre-Christian religious elements and to pan-Celtic religion in general. This paper is not Wiccan; it is from hereditary Welsh-Celtists. $3 for sample; quarterly; $9 US and Canada; $12 foreign airmail; US funds only: *The Bard*, 5102 N. 16th Dr., Lot 3, Phoenix, AZ 85015.

Circle Network News is a newspaper attuned to Paganism, Goddess ways, Shamanism, Magick, Nature Spirituality and related ways; includes rituals, articles, news, contacts, reviews, photos. $3.00 for sample; quarterly; $9.00 US; $13.00 US or Canada First Class; $17.00 elsewhere by air; US funds only: *Circle Network News*, P.O. Box 219, Mt. Horeb, WI 53572.

Council of the Magickal Arts newsletter provides a means of communication between various traditions; membership is open to anyone that practices magic in the light and love of the Goddess and/or God. $2.00 for sample; quarterly; $13 dues; $7.00 subscription without membership: Judy Causone, Editor, *Council of the Magickal Arts*, 9707 Chatfield St., Houston, TX. 77025.

Covenant of the Goddess Newsletter (COG) Craft and Pagan news, announcements, articles, poetry, and humor. Write for sample; 8 times a year; $15/year donation to be put on mailing list: *COG Newsletter*, P.O. Box 1226, Berkeley, CA 94704.

The Crone Papers is a participatory journal of Elder magick, power, and wisdom concentrating on the special magick of the older individual and dedicated to the exploration and understanding of the concept of the Crone in her magickal, religious, and wise-woman aspects. You don't have to be old and/or female to contribute. Two first class stamps for sample; eight times a year; $7.50 US; $14 outside US and Canada: *The Crone Papers*, P.O. Box 181, Crossville, TN 38557.

A Druid Missal-Any is the newsletter of the Reformed Druids of North America, Inc. It contains news of the various Groves (groups) around the country, articles about the Ancient Celts, philosophical debates among modern neo-Pagan Druids, customs, rituals, meditation exercises, changes in bylaws, and announcements. $1 for sample; 8 times a year; $4.50 US; $7.50 outside US: *A Druid Missal-Any*, 616 Miner Rd., Orinda, CA 94563.

The Druids' Progress is a journal of Ar nDraíocht Féin (ADF): A Druid Fellowship. Half consists of articles, essays, songs, and rituals by the Archdruid (Isaac Bonewits); half consists of similar materials produced by members, including comments on preceding issues. $5 for sample; semi-annual; $25 US; $35 US First Class, Canada and Mexico; $45 elsewhere (includes membership in ADF and *News from the Mother Grove*): *The Druid's Progress*, P.O. Box 1022, Nyack, NY 10960.

Earth First! The Radical Environmental Journal offers news and philosophy of the Earth First! Movement - biocentrism, deep ecology, monkeywrenching, civil disobedience, big wilderness. $2 for sample; 8 times a year; $15 US; $25 foreign surface, $40 airmail: *Earth First!*, P.O. Box 7, Canton, NY 13617.

The Faerie Folk Newsletter is a newsletter on the Welsh/Celtic tradition; it includes articles, poetry, recipes, and rituals on Wicca and metaphysics. $1 for sample; quarterly; $5 per year: *The Faerie Folk Newsletter*, P.O. Box 100585, Ft. Lauderdale, FL 33310.

Georgian Newsletter contains articles, poetry, events, editorials, news, and ads.

$1 for sample; monthly; $8 US; $16 (foreign surface) Canada; $32 elsewhere (airmail): *Georgian Newsletter*, 1908 Verde, Bakersfield, CA 93304.

Greener Times is the newsletter of Committees of Correspondence. It contains information about Green issues and events nationally, regionally, and locally. Quarterly: Committees of Correspondence, Dee Berry, Coordinator of Clearinghouse, P.O. Box 30208, Kansas City, MO 64112.

Harvest is a neo-Pagan journal devoted to bringing together the fruits of many traditions and belief systems as well as covering news of interest to the Pagan and Wiccan communities. Thought-provoking articles and letters, networking, reviews, rituals, songs, recipes, art, and poetry. $2 for sample; 8 times a year; $10 US; $13.50 US and Canada First Class; $18 elsewhere: *Harvest*, P.O. Box 228, S. Framingham, MA 01701.

Heartsong Review is a resource guide for New Age music of the Spirit, written by and for consumers. Includes detailed reviews of music in many styles and spiritual orientations. $4 for sample; semi-annual; $6/one year or $10/two years (foreign add $2): *Heartsong Review*, P.O. Box 1084, Cottage Grove, OR 97424.

Isian News is the magazine of the "Fellowship of Isis" and includes news of members, of the Fellowship and of other events of interest to members; lists temples, shrines, and centres associated with the Goddess; and lists members' publications, artistic works, crafts, etc. The magazine also includes articles on subjects of general interest to members. 1.30 pounds for sample (1.60 by air); quarterly; 5.00 pounds or $8 ($6.00 or $10.00 by air): The Fellowship of Isis, Clonegal Castle, Enniscorthy, Eire.

Moccasin Line; quarterly; $15 US and Canada; $25 overseas: *Moccasin Line*, Northwest Indian Women's Circle, P.O. Box 8279, Tacoma, WA 98408.

News from the Mother Grove announces ADF policies, local grove activities, lectures, and other appearances by the Archdruid. It is short and news-oriented. Bi-monthly; (see *Druids' Progress* above): *News from the Mother Grove*, P.O. Box 1022, Nyack, NY 10960.

Pagan Parents' League Newsletter contains letters, editorials, stories, book reviews, etc. by Pagan families for Pagan families, with a focus on parenting. Quarterly; sample free with contribution of postage stamps: *Pagan Parents' League*, P.O. Box 423-P, Bay Shore, NY 11706.

Pagana is the newsletter of the Pagan/Occult/Witchcraft Special Interest Group of American Mensa; non-Mensans are welcome as associate members. $2 per issue ($2.50 foreign air mail): *Pagana*, P.O. Box 9336, San Jose, CA 95157.

Pagans for Peace Newsletter is a networking newsletter for politically active radical Pagans, with news of environmental, Native, anarchist, feminist, lesbian, gay, and peace movements. Write for sample; monthly; $15 US (sliding scale on request, free to prisoners): *Pagans for Peace Newsletter*, P.O. Box 86134, North Vancouver, BC V7L 4J5, Canada.

Panegyria is a journal of Pagan interest about happenings in the Pacific Northwest US and beyond. Articles designed to stimulate thoughts from the Northwest's only public Pagan church organization. First Class postage for 3 ounces for sample; 8 times a year; $8 US; $12 US First Class; $16 overseas: *Panegyria*, P.O. Box 85507, Seattle, WA 98145.

The Pipes of PAN "is a journal of Pagans Against Nukes (PAN), an activist organisation dedicated to the banishment of nuclear technology from our Earth and the re-establishment of a culture that lives in harmony with Her. We seek to coordinate all Pagans, of whatever land and tradition, in political and magical work to achieve this end, that the Earth be Greened Anew." (Also includes "Pagan Parenting Network Newsletter.") $2 (in bills) for sample; 3 times a year; 4.00 pounds (surface); 7.00 pounds (air): *The Pipes of PAN*, 'Blaenberem,' Mynyddcerrig, Llanelli, Dyfed, Cymru (Wales) SA15 5BL, UK.

Potlatch is a newsletter created by Lee Allen. It provides current news and emerging trends in natural communities. Self-addressed, stamped envelope for sample; occasional; free: *Potlatch*, P.O. Box 4674, Chicago, IL 60680.

Shaman's Drum: A Journal of Experiential Shamanism is a publication of the Cross-Cultural Shamanism Network which is dedicated to fostering a shamanistic consciousness and to promoting understanding among various healing traditions, disciplines, and people. It contains articles, reviews, opinions, interviews, rituals, and resource listings. $15 US; $20 Canada; $24 overseas: *Shaman's Drum*, P.O. Box 2636, Berkeley, CA 94702.

Starlight is published by a Fellowship of Isis Centre/Grove. Articles on the Craft, Goddesses, poems, and short stories are included. *Starlight* is unique as the only Finnish pagan paper published in English. $2 for sample; quarterly; $8 (Printed Matter/Airmail); send only bills (no cheques): *Starlight*, c/o Sirius, P.O. Box 452, OO1O1 Helsinki, Finland.

The Sword of Dyrnwyn is the newsletter of: Y Tylwth Teg, 1029 Peachtree St. NE, Suite 218, Atlanta, GA 30309.

UNICORN, Magie, Schamanismus, Wege zur Erde, was for years the leading publication on Witchcraft, Paganism, magic, and shamanism in Germany. It ended with number 13. Since articles are still of interest, all issues have been consolidated into a Complete Edition in hardcover. Deutschmark (DM) 12 for single issue; DM 250 for complete edition: *Unicorn*, HORUS Buchhandlung, Bismarckstr. 19, D–5300, Bonn, West Germany.

The White Light contains information regarding ceremonial magick and related areas. $1.25 for sample; quarterly; $5 US; $8 overseas: *The White Light*, P.O. Box 93124, Pasadena, CA 91109.

Wiccan Rede is a English/Dutch, Pagan/occult magazine with in-depth articles on Craft heritage, Symbolism and Archetypal images, Nature and Natural Magic, etc. English summaries accompany the Dutch articles. $3 for sample (in bills); quarterly; $10 US airmail; 6 pounds UK; Dutch Guilders 18.50 Europe: *Wiccan Rede*, P.O. Box 473 - 3700 AL Zeist - Holland.

Wildfire (formerly *ManySmokes*) is a journal serving students and friends of Sun Bear and the Bear Medicine Society; includes articles on ecology, Native American paths, Earth awareness, art, reviews, and fiction. $2.50 for sample; semi-annual; $5/year: Bear Tribe Medicine Society, P.O. Box 9167, Spokane, WA 99209.

Wild Magic Bulletin is published by Elf Lore Family, P.O. Box 1082, Bloomington, IN 47402.

Wodenwood is a "generic" neo-Pagan journal which contains articles, stories, humor, and book reviews. $1.50 for sample; quarterly; $5/year: *Wodenwood*, P.O. Box 33284, Minneapolis, MN 55433.

Wood and Water is an eco-Pagan, Goddess-oriented, feminist-influenced magazine. $2 for sample; quarterly, 3.40 pounds; 6 pounds airmail; dollar equivalents please (no foreign checks or money orders): *Wood and Water*, 4, High Tor Close, Babbacombe Rd., Bromley, Kent BR1 3LQ, UK.

■ Music Resources

Ladyslipper Catalog is "the world's most comprehensive Catalog and Resource Guide of Records and Tapes by Women." This annotated catalog also includes songbooks, posters, and other goods. It is published annually by: Ladyslipper, Inc., P.O. Box 3124, Durham, NC 27715; write for copy. Artists include:

Alive! - "City Life," "Call it Jazz," and "Alive!"
Alix Dobkin - "Lavendar Jane Loves Women," "Living With Lesbians," "XX Alix," and "Never Been Better"
Catherine Madsen & Greater Lansing Spinsters Guild - "The Patience of Love"
Cyndee Grace - "Songs of the Goddess"
Debbie Fier - "Firelight" and "In Your Hands"
Karen Mackay - "West Virginia Woman" and "Annie Oakley Rides Again!"
Kay Gardner - "Mooncircles," "Emerging," "Fishersdaughter," "Moods & Rituals," "A Rainbow Path," "Avalon," and "Garden of Ecstasy"
Libana - "A Circle is Cast," "Libana, A Women's Chorus: Vol 1," "Libana, A Women's Chorus: Vol 2," and "Handed Down"
Ruth Barrett and Cyntia Smith - "Deepening" "Aeolus" & "Rolling World"
Willie Tyson - "Full Count," "Willie Tyson," and "Debutante"

Circle Network (P.O. Box 219, Mt. Horeb, WI 53572) has albums/tapes including:

Angie Remedi - "The Mother Calls"
Gwydion Pendderwen - "The Faerie Shaman" and "Gwydion Sings Songs for the Old Religion"
Jim Alan - "Dragon Tracks" and "Tales of the Songsmith"
Jim Alan and Selena Fox - "Circle Magick Musick" and "Songs of Pagan Folk"
Kenny and Tzipora Klein - "Dreamer's Web," "Moon Hooves in the Sand," and "Songs of the Otherworld"
Susan Arrow and the Quivers - "Welcome Sweet Pleasure"

Also see *Heartsong Review* and *The Gaia Catalog* in periodicals above.

■ Graphic and Fine Arts

Sudie Rakusin, *Dreams and Shadows: A Journal*. Amazon Images: 1987. and *Goddesses and Amazons: A Journal*. 1983.

■ Drama

Z. Budapest, *The Rise of the Fates*. Susan B. Anthony Coven #1: Los Angeles, 1976.
Pagan Kids Book. New Leaf Distribution, 5425 Turlane Dr. S.W. Atlanta, GA 30336

■ Notes

1. Jean Mountaingrove, personal correspondence, 1988.
2. *Goddess Rising*, Spring 1988, Issue 20, p. 2.
3. *Of a Like Mind*, Brochure, 1985.
4. *Woman of Power: a magazine of feminism, spirituality, and politics*, Issue 9—Nature, Spring 1988, Cover.
5. *SageWoman*, Fall 1986, Inside front cover.
6. Diane Mariechild, *Mother Wit*. Trumansburg, New York: The Crossing Press, 1981, pp. 62–63.
7. *The Bible*, New Scofield Reference Edition. New York: Oxford University Press, 1967, p. 99.
8. Selena Fox, "United for Liberty. . . A Special Report," *Circle Network News*, Winter 1985.
9. Fox.
10. "Pagan Strength Web," *Circle Network News*, Winter 1985.

CHAPTER 7

The Future
of
Feminist
Religion

Few people would have believed that by the year 2000 thousands of women would be defining themselves as Witches, but women's spirituality and feminist religion are growing. In the past several years, women new to the women's community and those who have been involved in women's issues for some time have been exploring their interest in Wicca and choosing to identify themselves as Witches. Feminist spirituality is alive and vibrant. Women are actively working to define for themselves what it means to be spiritual. They are looking for spiritual practices that affirm them as women and carry forth the values they found in the women's movement.

Past chapters have detailed where the women who comprise this community of womanspirit have come from, but little about why. Women involved in women's spirituality often seem to question what has drawn them toward an alternative religion. There does not seem to be an over-all answer to this question, but there do seem to be several common theories. Probably the theory which most often is heard is simply that there is a magic within the women themselves. It does seem that any time a group of women are allowed to interact freely, a special energy is generated. It is not hard to believe this theory if one has ever attended any large gathering of women. There is something different in the atmosphere. A level of freedom and understanding that is seldom found in the "outside" world. This is not to say everything is perfect, but there is a charge which seems to pass from woman to woman, whispering, "We are all one in the Goddess. We have a power which cannot be taken from us. You remember. . . you remember."

And they do remember. Those who believe in reincarnation say that perhaps they are tribes of Amazons who have all come back to live in this time. Others think the women who witnessed the fall of the great matriarchies have come back to insure the fall of the patriarchal system. Many women speak of memories of the burning times, while others remember the Holocaust. Memories of temples, shamans, and healers abound among these women who find themselves drawn to womanspirit. In the words of the Re-formed Congregation of the Goddess: "Our name was chosen to reflect the matriarchal origins of womyn's religion. Womyn's religion and womyn's culture are not new. Our name acknowledges that this is not the first time womyn have recognized the need to express their intuitive and spiritual selves in a supportive structure with other womyn. We are not beginning to find each other and our spiritual beliefs for the first time, but are re-membering and re-forming the ancient congregations of the Goddess."[1]

But if this is true, why now? Some feel that it is because of the dawning of the new age. Astrologically speaking, we are reported to be in a time of great change. We are currently on the cusp of a new astrological age. Not long ago most people would have had little understanding of what this meant, but with familiar songs about "The Dawning of the Age of Aquarius," and publicity about the Harmonic Convergence (interpreted as the start of this new age on several calendars including the Mayan and Hopi), most people have some idea that we are supposed to be entering a new astrological period.

The astrological age changes every 2,000 years, and we are currently thought to be on the cusp between the Piscean Age and the Aquarian Age. Unlike linear time, astrological time is not perceived to change suddenly. Each change is marked by a period in which there is thought to be a blending of the energies of the old sign and the new. A cusp is such a time. The influences of the Aquarian Age are said to have been affecting our thought since the beginning of this century. Although, according to astrologers, it is only now that we are either living in the cusp of the Aquarian Age, or in the Aquarian Age itself (depending on which astrologer you ask).

These astrological theories are supported by a comparison of the attributes of Pisces and Aquarius in view of our world culture. The Piscean Age was concerned with duality, and many of the issues we currently struggle with are thought to stem from Piscean concepts.

Pisces caused people to be concerned with differences while Aquarius looks for similarities. The following lists compare the attributes of both ages:

Piscean	Aquarian
Duality	Equality
Spirit outside	Spirit within
God as authority figure	Oneness with all life
Required middle-man between God & the people	Personal responsibility
Good vs. Evil	No need for blame
God vs. Devil	No concept of external evil
Following orders	Honoring inner truth
Rulers as authority figures	True government by the people
Rulers high/people low	Quiet organic revolutions
Hierarchy, monarchy, and bureaucracy	Government by inner authority
Allegiance, nationalism, patriotism	Loyality to self
Spirituality high/sexuality low	Love includes sex
Man high/woman low	Equality of the sexes
Racism	Integration and equality
Exploitation of the planet	Ecology
Travel by water	Travel by air
Getting high on liquids (alcohol)	Getting high with air (marijuana)
Communication with liquids (ink)	Communication through air (TV, radio)[2]

As Marion Weinstein points out in *Positive Magic*, many of the challenges which we are experiencing now are due to the cusp phenomenon: oil, coal or other (Piscean) energy companies which are still exploiting natural resources, using advertising campaigns to pass as ecologically sound; rigidly structured forms of meditation; sexual exploitation; communes run by one person; enlightenment for a fee; transference of old religious feeling to newer ideologies, such as psychiatry.[3]

A cusp is alive with change. Systems and institutions which have been in place for generations are questioned, and new ones are erected in their place. It is said those living in the cusp assist in pre-setting the vibrations of the new age. Perhaps this is why so many women are drawn into what is clearly an Aquarian spiritual form. Women of spirit see the future. These women of spirit are the future. It seems that most astrologers feel there is an inevitability about the changes which occur at the beginning of a new age. There is little hope of erecting barriers which will enforce static situations. This causes me to feel that as we come more fully into the Age of Aquarius, there will probably be more women involved in feminist religions. I am not speaking of Christian reformation. I am speaking of an actual women's religion. Christianity is very clearly a Piscean religion, and the attempt to resurrect Christianity from its two thousand years of Piscean dogma is obviously a cusp phenomenon.

■ Visions of a Feminist Future

If we honor the ideas of women's thealogy, then we are responsible for creating our own future. The inevitability of change brought about by the Aquarian Age does not allow us to sit by and wait for the day when women are truly recognized as equal and when woman-centered religions are as common as the mainstream religions of today. In keeping with the thealogy of women's Wicca, it is important that we take an active part in envisioning and creating our future.

But how does one go about creating the future? Although there are many potential ways in which one can generate reality, perhaps one of the most accessible is through visualization. Visualization, as a part of women's Witchcraft, is an art. It requires that one understand where one is headed and that one be able to recognize both the end result which is wished for and the steps along the way. Visualization is one of the tools we have to assist us in ordering our reality.

There are several simple steps in visualization. The first of these involves determining the essence of what you want to occur and defining for yourself what you would like to become reality. Establish clearly in your mind what you want your reality to be. In terms of creating a feminist future, this may be something you wish to talk over with your women friends. Spend some time talking and creating in your mind what it would be like to live in a world where women were free to practice their religion as they pleased, where all women were free to be themselves in every area of their lives. What would it be like to get up in the morning? How would your day be different? How would women act toward each other? What would you do for a living, and what kind of space would you live in? How would your spirituality be a part of your life, and what would you do to honor and celebrate it? Hazy visions produce hazy results, so it is important to be clear about what it is you wish to accomplish.

The second step is to create images of these circumstances occurring. Make these images in whatever ways you normally express yourself. Make images in your mind, with your hands, with words and music; use all your senses to help you envision the world in a new way. When you have some clear ideas about this future, begin to create pictures of this new reality. In your mind make images, still pictures or movies; imagine yourself interacting with other people and your environment. Tell yourself stories about this future. Draw pictures of it. Make your pictures and stories as vivid as possible, and share your visions with your friends. Often it is helpful to visualize steps along the way. Setting an over-all goal is critical, but it is also important for most people to see their work is generating some results. Visualizing some short-term goals is one way to watch your energy as it manifests. Always keep your long-range goals in mind, but, when possible, break them down into the pieces that form the whole. Spend time figuring out how things would work in this new order and what would have to change for them to become acknowledged.

The third step is simply to think of these images often. Spend some time each day thinking about the future you wish to come into being. If you have a time of structured meditation or quiet, this would be a good time to include some thoughts about the new future that we are creating. If you do words of power, remember to include an articulation of your visions along with the rest of your spellwork. Whenever you find yourself with little to occupy your attention, focus on these visions. In the garden, stuck in a traffic jam, before you go to sleep, or any other quiet time is a space you can use to define and refine your visions of a future which includes womanspirit. As much as possible, act in accordance with your visions, as if they were already true. I am not advocating you do things that will make your current life difficult, but whenever it is feasible, bring your visions into the present moment and live as if reality had already changed. This is womanspirit in action, positive energy directed toward a shared goal.

It is important when working with visualization to remember some of the other points of women's Craft thealogy. Visualization is commonly used in many New Age philosophies; however, most often, few ethics are applied. Visualization which includes other people should acknowledge their free will. It is necessary when including others in your visualizations that your work end with a statement that this work is according to the free will of all and for the good of all. Although we have been specifically speaking of visualization in terms of creating a positive future for women of spirit, visualization is also applicable to any other areas of your life where it seems appropriate. If we can visualize what it is we wish to become true, we are well on our way to achieving this goal.

It is one of my fondest dreams to think of a future in which women, from the time they are children, are free to practice, learn, share, and explore their spiritual feelings. A world which knows no war, no hunger, and no exploitation of people, of nature, or of the earth. I envision a time when women of spirit are acknowledged, respected, and honored by their community. I delight in detailing the steps along the way and doing my part to assure that they come to be. May each woman dare to dream of such a future.

■ The Microcosm and the Macrocosm

In the thealogy of women's Wicca there is a belief that each individual helps create reality. Every woman who takes an interest in her spiritual development brings all women closer to a reality in which each woman is accepted, appreciated, and valued. Helping oneself helps others. This does not mean that one should not be concerned with the lives and actions of others, but it does mean that if we wish for positive change in the world, then the place to begin is with ourselves. If you wish for peace, live in peaceful ways. If you wish for more love in the world, act in loving ways. If each individual acts the way they wish the world to be, the world will become such a place. All women are helped each time any of us make a positive action.

This philosophy is based on an ancient occult concept of the microcosm and the macrocosm. In this belief, each individual is thought to comprise a tiny world. As individuals take certain actions in their little worlds, the larger world is affected. Marion Weinstein explains this concept in *Positive Magic*:

> "The Universe as Macrocosm: The Universe is comprised of harmony, the infinite and complete *unity* of all life. The Power is the lifeforce of the Universe, and in a sense synonymous with it. We are all inheritors of the Power, and the Power holds no favorites. It exists equally in everything and everyone; when we are in tune with it, we are in tune with the perfect balance of the Universe.
>
> "The Microcosm: That's each of us—that's the self. We are each individualizations of the Power, and anything the Power can do, we can do. The Power can create—worlds, stars, planets, babies—and we can create. The Universe is complete (it has everything it needs), and we are complete (we potentially have everything we need). We have the infi-

nite resources of the Power to bring about the work of positive magic, to make our potential into reality."[4]

This concept of the microcosm and the macrocosm is based in sympathetic magic. Sympathetic magic is one of the oldest and most common magical forms. If one lights a candle in hopes that it will "illuminate" her thinking, this is sympathetic magic. Sympathetic magic is reflected in the saying, "As below, so above" (whatever is happening on the earth plane is mirrored in the less-commonly-perceived realm). If we follow this theory to its logical conclusion, then each one of us is helping to create reality. Not only the forms and circumstances in which we find ourselves, but also in all of the minute details which comprise all life here on Earth. Each of our actions, great and small, contributes to creating our portion of the entire universe. This may seem hard to fathom until we remember one of the most basic concepts of women's magic and thealogy—that we are each Goddess. We are the creators and the destroyers. As such, the future is in our hands. We can create the world we want. By knowing and choosing what we wish reality to be, women of spirit can influence the world.

Spiritual women have embarked on a long journey, and we have not always chosen the easy path. There is very little in the patriarchal system which surrounds us that supports us and our decision to travel on this road. The path is shrouded in mystery and illusion which we must each unravel to reach the truth. There are suggestions of which way to travel, but no rules about how to proceed. Those who are wise learn to use the systems which give hints and point the way. Our journey is not all struggle; along the way we often stop to celebrate and honor both each other and the Mother who gives us life. We are creating a new world. We celebrate this emerging reality and ourselves in new ways while we journey to a form of spiritual practice which truly reflects women's spirituality. And we do not journey alone. Thousands of our sisters are walking with us. Each wishing "To Know" one another.

▪ Recommended Reading

Shakti Gawain, *Creative Visualization*. Mill Valley, California: Whatever Publishing, 1978.

■ *Notes*

1. "Developing Dianic Wicca" conference brochure, Re-formed Congregation of the Goddess, 1988.

2. Marion Weinstein, *Positive Magic: Occult Self-Help*. Custer, Washington: Phoenix Publishing Co., 1981, abstracted from pp. 20–24.

3. Weinstein, pp. 22–23.

4. Weinstein, p. 211.